FOOD IN EARLY GREECE

BY

KENTON FRANK VICKERY

ARES PUBLISHERS INC.
CHICAGO   MCMLXXX

VITA

Kenton Frank Vickery was born in Riverton, Iowa, February 9, 1904. He was graduated with the degree of Bachelor of Arts from Augustana College, Rock Island, Illinois, in 1925. He was awarded a scholarship for the next academic year in the Graduate School of the University of Illinois, where he received the degree of Master of Arts in 1926. He continued his graduate studies at the University of Illinois, while teaching with the rank of Assistant in Classics, until 1929, when he became Instructor in Classical Languages at Northwestern University. In 1930 he returned to the University of Illinois as a Fellow in Classics, to prepare a dissertation in completion of the requirements for the degree of Doctor of Philosophy.

Exact Reprint of the Edition:
Urbana, 1936.
Ares Publishers Inc.
612 North Michigan Avenue
Chicago, Illinois 60611
Printed in the United States of America
International Standard Book Number
0-89005-339-1

PREFACE

The title of this study, *Food in Early Greece,* requires, perhaps, some explanation. The expression *Early Greece* refers, chronologically, to the time previous to the end of the Bronze Age and, geographically, to mainland Greece, Macedonia, the Troad, Crete, and the other Aegean islands. In the almost complete absence of literary records, I have based my work largely on archaeological evidence, and to a lesser extent on that of language.

The original reports of all archaeological research coming within the scope of my plan, and many other studies based on them, I have carefully read and excerpted, making note of all references to the discovery of the remains of, or pictorial representations of, edible plant products and animals, wild and domestic. I have also made note of all the available facts about the discoveries which aid in placing the articles chronologically, geographically, and ethnologically. The facts so gathered I have systematically presented in such a way that, as I hope, they may prove useful to others who may later work with the same material, and thus have a value independent of that of the conclusions based upon them. In regard to the latter, I have sought to determine: (1) what food products were known to the peoples of the various regions of the Aegean in each period of prehistory; (2) what was the relative importance of each sort of food in the diet of those peoples; (3) to what extent food products were articles of trade and transport; and (4) how food was prepared. Many questions in regard to these matters remain unanswered; I believe, however, that I have made some substantial contribution to the general fund of knowledge about Greece in the Bronze Age. My investigations cover thoroughly those books and periodicals available in 1931, at which time the dissertation was originally written and, somewhat less thoroughly, those which appeared between then and the summer of 1933.

This work, which is intended as the first of a series of studies on food among the peoples of the ancient Mediterranean, was prepared under the direction of Dr. W. A. Oldfather, of the University of Illinois, who first directed my attention to this field of investigation, and to whom I take this opportunity to express my gratitude for his interest and guidance. I also wish to extend my thanks to Dr. George E. Mylonas, of Washington University, who read the manuscript and made a number of apt criticisms, by the aid of which I revised the work in the final form sent to press.

KENTON F. VICKERY

Lock Haven, Pennsylvania
March 13, 1936

CONTENTS

I
THE AEGEAN REGION AND ITS ENVIRONS

In the course of the extensive excavations in the Aegean area and the nearby regions, that is, in the Troad, in mainland Greece, on the Cyclades, and in Crete, remains of human food have frequently come to light. Through the study of these in the light of such additional information as can be thrown on the matter by the remains of household utensils, the representations of edible plants, animals, and the like in art, and by linguistic study, it is possible to learn what were the food resources of the peoples of the prehistoric Aegean region and, within limits, to learn what articles they already had in Neolithic times and what they acquired or learned to use later. Since, however, the Neolithic Age is separated from historic times by long ages during which the relations between the subdivisions of the region, later the seat of Hellenic civilization, changed greatly, it is necessary to map out carefully each important geographical and chronological division and to study the cultural relations between the various regions. By doing so one becomes able to make reasonable inferences from the various finds—to decide, for example, whether the remains of olive oil on an island of the Cyclades justify the conclusion that the Cretans of a given age cultivated the olive and used oil.

Most of the geographical divisions of the Aegean are represented by sites yielding remains of food or other significant finds. One group of sites clusters in central Macedonia and Thrace; another is in the Troad; a third is in Chalcidice; another is in the Peneus Valley and around the Pagasian Gulf; still another group is found in the Spercheius Valley and Boeotia. Southern mainland Greece was an important part of the Aegean world; Crete was the center of the highest form of Aegean civilization throughout the greater part of the Copper and Bronze ages. Still other important sites are found on various islands of the Cyclades. Although, being definitely prehistoric, the cultures on these sites are not directly datable, it is possible to establish chronological series through the study of ceramic remains in each culture area; then these series may be correlated; finally approximate dates may be fixed for them through correlating them with datable series in lands possessing written history—notably with those of Egypt. Thus the chronology of the entire Aegean region and its environs is roughly known.

In general, the cultural development of the various regions went through four stages: Neolithic, and Early, Middle, and Late periods of the Age of Metals. Of the first of these, the Neolithic, the beginnings cannot be dated. Neolithic remains have been discovered in every region of culture in the area except the Cyclades and the Troad, but the most important group of Neolithic stations, considering the development of the culture and the extent of the data available, is that in the Peneus Valley and around the Pagasian Gulf. Here are found the important sites Dimini and Sesklo, the stratification of which furnished the basis for the Thessalian pottery series. There is some evidence that this culture was not indigenous, but that it entered Greece from the North, being perhaps related to the Tripolje culture of southern Russia. Its relations to the Neolithic culture of Crete, if it was related to it at all, are not established.

The end of Neolithic culture seems to have resulted from intrusion from without. In some places it was entirely displaced by a new culture using metal implements; this occurred in Macedonia, Chalcidice, in the Spercheius Valley, and to the South. In Thessaly, although the intrusion did not end the old civilization, it was followed by a serious decline; in Crete the Metal Age culture which developed can scarcely be compared with the Neolithic owing to the paucity of remains, but it seems to have been somewhat different, to say the least. It has been generally believed that the Cyclades were first extensively settled at the beginning of the Age of Metals, and by people who brought with them, as we shall see, the common domestic animals *by water*. That they may have brought new articles of food to other parts of the Aegean world as well is quite obvious. Thus we are brought to a fundamental principle in the interpretation of the archaeological evidence: *articles of food known in Neolithic times in a given area of the Aegean world may fairly be supposed to have continued in use in the later periods, but those known only from discoveries datable as post-Neolithic may not be assumed to have been known earlier.* It is also established that things as bulky as domestic animals could be transported by sea in the Early Age of Metals.

Were the source of the new elements introduced at this time known beyond controversy, we could draw more inferences about conditions in one part of the Aegean world from the known facts about another part. The orthodox view, accepted by Sir Arthur Evans, Eduard Meyer, and H. R. Hall, sees Anatolia as the source of an immigration that peopled the Cyclades, replaced the earlier cultures in most of mainland Greece, and played a large part in the movement which resulted in the Cretan Neolithic civilization becoming Early Minoan.[1] A form of this view is clearly set forth in Frankfort.[2] Recently, however, Matz[3] has contended that Anatolia is only incidentally involved in the movement, and he seeks

[1]Cf. Blegen, *Zygouries*, p. 210.
[2]*Studies in the Early Pottery of the Near East*, 2, pp. 85 ff.
[3]*Frühkretischen Siegel*, pp. 26 ff. and 246 ff.

its source in the North and Northwest—in the Danube country and the Balkans. He minimizes the connection between Crete and Egypt in the Early Minoan Age, and disputes the existence of an ethnic connection between Early Helladic and Early Cycladic culture.[1*] Whatever the ultimate conclusion may be, however, we may at least claim some community of culture between the various parts of the Aegean World, including Anatolia, in the Early Age of Metals, and a considerable community of culture in the southern part—that is, between Crete, the Cyclades, and the area to which the term Early Helladic is applied.[2*]

While cultural unity between Macedonia, the Troad, etc., and the southern Aegean cannot be claimed, it has now been determined that Troy I and II and Macedonian A represent essentially the same period, and that as a result of commerce, if not of ethnic connection, they constitute two phases of the same culture. It is probable, moreover, that more complete research will permit one to include Thrace in this culture area.[3*] The Troad, and especially the mound of Hissarlik, was the first part of this region to be explored;[4*] recently Macedonia also has been the scene of extensive and systematic excavation. Remains dating from Neolithic times to the end of the Bronze Age have come to light, and chronological series based on ceramics have been established, known as Macedonian A, B, and C, and identified as approximate Macedonian equivalents of the Early, Middle, and Late periods of other series.

The Early Period of the Age of Metals extended over a very long time. It is difficult to set an exact date for its end. Although it certainly did not end at exactly the same time throughout the Aegean region, the Middle Period is roughly contemporary in each part. The end of the Early Helladic Age seems well marked. A widespread destruction appears to have occurred, resulting in the appearance of a distinctly different culture. It is very probable that this new culture resulted from the immigration of a new people, but to suppose that the older population and its civilization was entirely displaced is to presume too much. Throughout a large part of the Cyclades the Early Cycladic civilization disappeared; on some of the islands, however, it survived and developed along new lines, justifying for the new form of culture the name Middle Cycladic. In Crete the line between Early and Middle Minoan is harder to draw. It seems, indeed, that were the chronological system to be remade now, Early Minoan III, or a part of it, might be included in Middle Minoan I. Among the reasons for supposing this is the fact that the use of true bronze first began somewhat before the end of the Early Minoan Period, and that the building of the palaces and the making of polychrome ware seem to have begun in Early Minoan III.[5*] In the

---
*Numbers followed by the asterisk and enclosed in parentheses refer to notes at the end of the section; see page 14.

Troad and Macedonia some important movements took place. Troy II was destroyed, and there may have been an emigration from the Troad to Macedonia. Influences directly from the North also appear there.

What caused these changes? A correct answer to this question would enable one to make confident statements about the source of the new elements in Aegean culture appearing now for the first time. Unfortunately, as in the case of the similar problem in connection with the end of the Neolithic Age, the answer has not been given. There is reason, according to Heurtley,[4] for believing that the new ethnic elements in mainland Greece and their characteristic Minoan ware came from Asia Minor. Many excellent authorities affirm that the Hellenic-speaking peoples first entered Greece at this time, bringing new cultural elements into the Aegean area from without. Beloch[5] accepts the entry of Indo-European speaking peoples into the region of the Axios in the beginning or middle of the third millenium, whence they spread during the following centuries. Meyer[6] confidently set 2000 B.C. as the latest date for the coming of the Greeks, but later he accepted a more conservative view.[6a] Buck[7] set 1600 B.C. as the date of their coming. Blegen,[8] on the other hand, regards 1900 B.C. as a better date for their coming than 1600, since the former date corresponds to the cultural break at the beginning of Middle Helladic I, whereas there is no break at the latter date. Whatever conclusion may finally be reached, we must deal with the likelihood that new elements of all sorts may have entered the Aegean world at the beginning of the Middle Bronze Age. On the other hand, the northern Aegean and the southern did not acquire any degree of unity of culture until the beginning of the Late Bronze Age.

The Middle Period of the prehistoric Aegean was not very long— not so long as the modern history of America. It was followed by another comparatively short, but culturally very important age, which we may call the Late Period of the Bronze Age, comprising Late Minoan, Late Cycladic, Late Helladic, Macedonian C, and Troy VI. A large part of the important archaeological discoveries of the Aegean Copper and Bronze ages belongs to this period. Its latter part belongs to literary tradition through the Greek epic, and much of Greek myth may have its roots in it.[9] For Crete the age naturally divides into two periods— namely, Middle Minoan III (in part, at least), and Late Minoan I and II; and Late Minoan III, corresponding to Late Helladic III, when the center of Aegean civilization shifted to the mainland, and Crete became part of

[4] *Antiquity* 1929, p. 320.
[5] *Griechische Geschichte* I¹, 2nd ed., p. 71.
[6] *G. des A.* I², 2, p. 721.
[7] *Classical Philology* 1926, p. 26.
[8] *A.J.A.* 1928, p. 154.
[9] See Nilsson, *The Minoan-Mycenaean Religion*, pp. 44 ff.

the Mycenaean world. The inclusion of at least a part of Middle Minoan III in the Late Period is well founded. Evans[10] states that the new era began in Middle Minoan III, and he[11] dates the Temple Repositories as Middle Minoan III.[7*] During the former part of the period Cretan influence spread to mainland Greece and became so strong that Evans vigorously objects to the use of the term Late Helladic at all.[12] We may from now on regard Crete and mainland Greece as one culture area. Another important development of this age is the bringing of the northern and southern Aegean into closer contact.[13]

There can be no question that there was a strong interaction of cultures within the Aegean region during this period, so that it is reasonable to generalize for the entire area conclusions reached about any particular part of it. It is not, however, certain how much the region may have been influenced from without. The commercial activity within the Aegean was so great that it is likely that many articles were imported from all lands bordering on the sea, and perhaps from far beyond through caravan trade. There may also have been considerable peaceful immigration from without—for example, from Egypt and Syria. Dörpfeld has proposed a Phoenician invasion of Crete during Middle Minoan III, but the theory has received little support.[14] He also once maintained that the country was then conquered by Achaeans from the mainland, but this theory has been definitely refuted.[15] There remains the possibility that the Greeks may have entered the Aegean area at the beginning of the Late Helladic Age.[16] In any case, we must again deal with the probability that at the beginning of the Late Period, as at the beginning of the Early and Middle periods of the Bronze Age, extensive new elements may have entered the Aegean world.

These, then, are the principles on which interpretation of the evidence will rest:

(1) Conclusions for earlier periods are valid for later ones, but those for later periods are not valid for earlier ones.

(2) As early as the beginning of the Early Bronze Age bulky articles, including domestic animals, could be transported by sea.

(3) Extensive influxes of new elements came to the Aegean world at the beginning of each new period of the Age of Metals.

---

[10]*P. of M.* 2, p. vi, note 1.
[11]*B.S.A.* 9, pp. 151 ff.
[12]See *Shaft Graves of Mycenae*, p. 49.
[13]Cf. Heurtley in *B.S.A.* 27, p. 59; *ibid.* 29, p. 177; and *Antiquity* 3, p. 322.
[14]*M.A.I.* 50, p. 80; cf. Meyer in *G. des A.* 2¹, pp. 164-165, where he acknowledged the possibility of an invasion, but denied permanent settlement or Semitic origin for the art of Middle Minoan III.
[15]See article by Karo in *P.W.*, *s.v. Kreta*.
[16]See Buck, *Classical Philology* 1926, p. 26; Blegen in *A.J.A.* 1928, p. 154; and Meyer in *G. des A.* 2¹, 2, p. 221, note 1, cited above.

(4) From the Early Bronze Age to the end of the Middle Bronze Age the North and the South each had considerable inner unity, but there is no evidence of extensive mutual interchange of culture elements between them.

(5) During the last period the Aegean world became increasingly close-knit, and the North and South, moreover, came into close contact.

NOTES

1. It is just possible that a searching zoological study of the remains of domestic animals in each region might help solve the problems.

2. Blegen (*A.J.A.* 43(1928), p. 149) states: "From the archaeological evidence now available for the first division it can now be confidently stated that the Early Minoan, Early Cycladic, and Early Helladic civilizations are all branches of one great parent stock, which pursued parallel, but more or less independent courses."

3. On the relations of the Troad to Macedonia see *Antiquity* 3(1929), p. 320; *B.S.A.* 29(1927-1928), pp. 178-181; and *B.S.A.* 27(1925-1926), pp. 51 and 64.

4. The identification of Hissarlik with Homeric Troy, which is still a matter of controversy (see C. Vellay, *Les nouveaux Aspects de la Question de Troie*, Paris, 1930), is of no consequence in the present problem.

5. See *P. of M.* 1, pp. 106 and 111; Hall, *Bronze Age*, p. 67; and Glotz, *Civilisation égéenne*, p. 25.

6. *Op. cit.*, 2¹, 2, p. 221, note 1: ". . . einstweilen erscheint hier noch Zuruckhaltung geboten."

7. Cf. also Hall (*Bronze Age*, pp. 109 and 179); and Meyer, *G. des A.* 2¹, p. 165, note 1, where the matter is stated succinctly and controversially.

II

ARCHAEOLOGICAL EVIDENCE: CRETE

The cultural center of the prehistoric Aegean in its most flourishing age, and one of the chief sources of our knowledge of that age is Knossós, the capitol of Minos. By a strange coincidence the first modern excavation there was carried out, in 1878, by Minos Kalokairinos, who discovered some painted pottery and some pithoi containing beans and peas.[1] The thorough-going excavation and partial restoration of the great structures on the site were begun by A. J. Evans just before the beginning of the present century, and have been going on more or less continuously ever since.[2] Among the finds bearing more or less on the subject of food are remains of grains, vegetables, and a very few of animals; numerous seal-stones, signets, and seal impressions; frescoes; and pottery with plant, animal, and marine designs. The reports give the impression of being complete so far as vegetable foods are concerned. Remains of wheat, barley, beans, and olives were found, sometimes in considerable quantity. Almost no mention is made of animal remains. The heads of *urus* oxen, so-called, found in the *House of the Sacrificed Oxen,* and the stag-horns found with the Snake Goddess collection are among the few references made to finds of a zoological character. C. Keller, however, during a visit to Knossos, found some animal remains, including some horns and skulls of the animal he describes as *Bos primigenius,*[1*] which he believed, from the circumstances of their discovery, to have belonged to animals which were stabled in the palace at the time it was destroyed.[2*] The wheat found stored on the floor of a room (the North Room of the Lapidary's Workshop) had apparently been in no container. In the South Room was found one pot containing beans of a sort identified by the workmen as of a kind now imported from Egypt and known as κυκιά μισιριωτικά, and another pot containing beans of a smaller variety.[3] The barley, which was found in the structure called the Caravanserai,[4] seems to have been kept in wooden bins. Evans' conjecture that it may have been used as animal feed finds support in the evidence of the use of barley for that purpose on the island of Thera (see page 27, below). The olive-stones, of Late Minoan III date, were found in the spring-chamber at the Caravanserai together with other remains of food.[5]

---

*Numbers followed by the asterisk and enclosed in parentheses refer to notes at the end of the section; see page 23.
[1]*B.C.H.* 4(1880), pp. 124 ff.; *B.S.A.* 6, p. 21.
[2]Part of the original publication of the finds is to be found in *B.S.A.,* vols. 6-11. Some of the material was published for the first time in the volumes of the *Palace of Minos.* For a somewhat detailed bibliography to 1914 see Fimmen, *Kretisch-mykenische Kultur,* p. 20.
[3]*B.S.A.* 7, p. 21; *P. of M.* 2, p. 54.
[4]*P. of M.* 2, p. 105.
[5]*Ibid.,* pp. 134-135.

Both the ox-heads and the stag-horns were found in unmistakable cult context.[6] The deer-horns are said to be those of the roe deer. Fish bones found in a cooking-pot furnish direct evidence of the use of fish as food.[7]

It will be noted that these discoveries belong to the Late Bronze Age—Middle Minoan III and later. The other discoveries on this site which aid in the study of food are chiefly of Neolithic date. Most of them were made in two Neolithic houses under the central court of the palace. Unlike later Cretan houses, these had fixed hearths. The ability of the Neolithic Cretans to make large pottery is demonstrated by the discovery on this site of a caldron over 70 cm. in diameter. Other significant finds were spindle-whorls and winders for yarn (proof, were any needed, of the domestication of sheep); figurines of the female human type (suggesting the worship of Mother Earth and, hence, agriculture), and animal figurines; bones of animals, including goats, short-horned cattle, and swine; sea shells, including cockles, large limpets, and whelks; and miscellaneous domestic pottery. C. Keller believed that he recognized also a bone of the *Bos primigenius*.[3*] Another interesting object, which seems to be contemporary with the Neolithic house in which it was found, was an almond seed surprisingly well preserved.

The cemeteries at Gournès and Maurospelio, near Knossos, have yielded some remains of the Middle Period. In addition to pottery, several seal-stones were discovered, with such subjects represented on them as wild goats, bulls, and a cow with her calf. Some of the seals from the site belong to the Middle Period, and some to the Late. The only pertinent object from the Maurospelio cemetery definitely dated as Middle Minoan is a Middle Minoan II seal-stone with a goat's-head design. A pit in the floor of one of the graves contained undated knuckle-bones of sheep and of goats. A jasper gem bearing the design of a flying fish was discovered in one of the tombs, undated, but certainly Minoan.

The Zapher Papoura tombs date from Late Minoan II-III, whereas tombs from the earliest part of the Late Period (Middle Minoan III), and some material of Middle Minoan II date were found in the cemetery at Maurospelio. The Royal Tomb of Isopata dates from Middle Minoan III and Late Minoan I. The Tomb of the Double Axes dates from Late Minoan I and II.[4*] Among the finds in these tombs the principal interest, so far as the study of food is concerned, is in the art: seal-stones and painted pottery, including clay coffins or larnakes, and the like. Among the utensils from the tombs at Zapher Papoura were movable hearths which, however, probably were not kitchen utensils, and some

[6] *Ibid.*, pp. 301 ff. and fig. 475.
[7] *B.S.A.* 7, p. 10; *P. of M.* 1, p. 555.

copper vessels which, in Evans' opinion, are frying pans. These form a part of a collection of bronze vessels from Tomb 14;[8] similar ones were found in Tomb 31, in a tomb at Mycenae,[9] and at Phaestos.[10] They are shaped like small skillets having a thin upright handle forming an extension of the rim. The one from Zapher Papoura is 10 cm. in diameter; the one from Phaestos is 11.5 cm. in diameter, 2.2 cm. deep, and 8.5 cm. high to the end of the handle. Among other vessels from Tomb 14 are a bronze lamp, pots, caldrons, and a vessel on three high legs.

Somewhat east of Gournès is the town site of Nirou Chani. Xanthoudides' excavations there exposed a structure of Late Minoan I date.[11] In the storage rooms (numbers 26 and 30 on the plan) were discovered remains of beans and perhaps of vetches. Among the other finds are stone lamps, a piece of fresco painting with part of picture that may be that of a wild goat, and bricks bearing the imprint of a goat's hoof. The significance of the site for the study of Minoan religion has been pointed out at length by Evans.[12] In the mountains southeast of Gournès is a sacred cave known as Psychro Cave.[5*] The results of the investigations there carried out by D. G. Hogarth have been published.[13] Although the stratified remains in the cave were deposited over an age extending from Middle Minoan times into the post-Minoan era, they belong largely to the Late Minoan Period. Boyd Dawkins examined the animal bones and recognized those of goats, swine, fallow deer, and oxen of the Cretan short-horned variety, which he termed *Bos creticus*.[14]

After Knossos, one of the most famous Cretan sites is Phaestos. Like Knossos, Phaestos was inhabited from Neolithic times to the end of the Minoan Age. The excavations there were conducted by the Italian Archaeological Mission in Crete, and were begun about the same time that Evans began his at Knossos.[6*]

The excavations at Phaestos revealed a palace similar to that at Knossos. As at Knossos, the latest palace was built over the ruins of an earlier one, and incorporated part of the earlier buildings in its structure. The earliest palace at Hagia Triada dates[15] from Middle Minoan III. Near these sites Minoan cemeteries have been found and excavated. The finds in the palaces and tombs of this group are similar to those discovered at Knossos. The discovery of animal bones in the palace was

---

[8] *Archaeologia* 59, p. 424.
[9] *Eph.* 1888, plates 9, 24, and p. 137.
[10] *M.A.* 14, p. 544 and fig. 29.
[11] *Eph.* 1922, pp. 1 ff.
[12] *P. of M.* 2, p. 279.
[13] *B.S.A.* 6, pp. 94 ff.
[14] *Memoirs and Proceedings of the Manchester Literary and Philosophical Society* 46(1902), p. xlviii. Cf. *S.M.*, p. 206.
[15] Karo, *R.V.G.*, *sub Hagia Triada*, sets its construction toward the end of M.M. III.

reported, but no attempt seems to have been made to identify them
exactly. Likewise the carbonized grain found there does not seem to have
been identified, but the reports do name, giving the place of discovery
and the context, some vegetables and fruits, including chick peas, dried
figs, and almonds. These were found in the magazines of the palace
at Hagia Triada.[16] In connection with them were discovered some bones
of small animals, described as the remains of food. In a larnax in one
of the tombs were found some olive-stones, and the remains of a food
containing bones.[17] A stone structure in the palace at Phaestos was
identified as an olive press.[18]

In order to learn something of the Neolithic settlement on the site,
the excavators sunk twenty-seven pits to virgin soil on the south slope
of the Acropolis. In more than half of them large quantities of animal
bones were found. Although Mosso, in his article on the Neolithic discoveries at Phaestos, gave a brief list of the animals represented, he has,
so far as I know, never published the full report of them as he intended.
C. Keller, however, investigated them, and revealed a very interesting
fact.[7*] He discovered that the unique horned sheep and short-horned
cattle still common in Crete were already raised in Neolithic times.

The site of Hagia Triada, already referred to, lies a short distance
north of Phaestos. A tholos tomb on this site dates from the very beginning of the Early Minoan Age and was in use throughout the
period.[8*] Large quantities of seal-stones bearing pictures of wild and
domestic animals have been discovered here and elsewhere in similar
tombs throughout the plain of Mesarà, dating, for the most part, from
Early Minoan III.[9*] Some rhytons from the tombs of Mesarà representing long-horned bulls constitute the earliest representations of these animals in Cretan art. They are definitely dated by Evans[19] as Middle
Minoan Ia; Xanthoudides[20] dated some of them Early Minoan III to
Middle Minoan I. In some of these tombs lamps showing signs of flame
about the mouth and belonging to the Middle Period have been found.
These are of some interest in the study of food, for they suggest the use
of olive oil in Crete at that date. Vegetable or animal remains very
seldom have been discovered in tombs in this region.

A Neolithic cave dwelling was discovered at Miamù, a site near the
sea southeast of Phaestos. The floor of the cave was found to be covered
with a deep black deposit containing bones of goats, sheep, cattle, hares,
and rabbits; a piece of stag-horn; sea shells; and the antennae of crabs
and lobsters. A quern and rubber, some pottery, and quantities of sherds

---

[16]*Mem. r. Ist. lomb.* 21, p. 244.
[17]*M.A.* 14, p. 635; *R.A.L.* 11, p. 321.
[18]*R.A.L.* 16, p. 290.
[19]*P. of M.* 3, p. 205.
[20]*Vaulted Tombs of Mesarà*, pp. 40-62.

were also among the finds. The Neolithic dating of the deposit, questioned by Montelius,[21] is maintained by Karo.[22]

In the hills a short distance from Phaestos is the Kamares Cave, so called from the nearby village of the same name. Some pottery found there in 1884 by a shepherd and recognized by archeologists as pre-Mycenaean came to be known as Kamares ware and, later, as Middle Minoan II polychrome ware. A. Taramelli and F. Halbherr visited the grotto in 1894; the former published[23] an account of their explorations, in which he stated that he had found the bones of goats and the skull of an ox, which he believed, however, to have been washed into the grotto. The cave was later systematically excavated by British archeologists, and the results were published by R. M. Dawkins and M.L.W. Laistner.[24] In one place in the cave the remains of "wheat or some other grain" were found among the sherds. It is unfortunate that the date of the pottery accompanying the grain is not given, for so far no dated remains of grain earlier than Middle Minoan III have been reported in Crete (some Late Minoan I pottery was found in the cave). It is also unfortunate that the exact nature of the grain could not be determined, for, whatever its date, it was placed in the cave in the observance of what must have been an already ancient cult.

The site of Tylissos, one of the most important in Crete for the study of food, lies a little northwest of Knossos.[10a] The remains of animals were carefully collected and submitted to Professor C. Keller of Zurich (who also examined the remains found at Phaestos and Knossos). Hatzidakis gives the following table of the animals identified, classifying them chronologically.

Middle Minoan	Late Minoan I	Late Minoan II
Bos primigenius	Bos primigenius	Bos primigenius
Bos brachycerus	Bos brachycerus	Bos brachycerus
Bos domesticus	. . . .	Bos primigenius et brachycerus
Capra aegagrus creticus	Capra aegagrus creticus	Capra aegagrus creticus
Capra domesticus	. . . .	Capra hiscius
Sus scrofa ferus	. . . .	Sus scrofa ferus
Sus domesticus indicus	. . . .	Sus domesticus indicus
	Cervus elaphus	Cervus elaphus
	Ovis aries palustris	Ovis aries palustris
	Equus caballus	Equus asinus
	Canis creticus	

As to the relative importance of the various animals represented, Hatzidakis says that there were thirty-two jaws of sheep and goats—

[21] La Grèce Préclassique, p. 9.
[22] R.V.G., s.v. Kreta.
[23] American Journal of Archaeology 1901, pp. 437 ff.
[24] B.S.A. 19, pp. 1 ff.

wild and domesticated, as compared with 17 jaws of swine—wild and domesticated; a proportion which, in his opinion, showed a relatively greater consumption of pork than that of Crete today.[25] C. Keller[26] says that sheep were the most numerous animals represented at Tylissos, followed closely by swine; goats were much less numerous, and cattle less numerous still. Hatzidakis says à propos of the so-called *Bos primigenius* that horns of these animals had been found of which the tips had been cut off; among these were included horns of both young and old.[27] It is stated that no bones of birds were found. A number of sea shells, including the common edible shellfish, were discovered. In addition, a large fish vertebra weighing 3-4 kilograms is said to have been found. Other finds on the site of Tylissos pertinent to the study of food include a number of seal-stones and sealings, some pottery with designs of animals and sea life, and some cooking utensils.

On the coast east of Knossos and northeast of the Psychro Cave lies Mallia, a site very important from the point of view of the student of Cretan antiquities.[11*] Its importance is due, not to its having been more important than Knossos, although it is true that the latter had not yet acquired its later importance, but to the preservation there of an earlier phase of construction than has been preserved on the other sites. The existing structure seems to have been built in Middle Minoan I; the site was occupied as early as Early Minoan I or II. It appears to have been abandoned during Middle Minoan II, and to have been reoccupied in Middle Minoan III. Thus any finds datable earlier than the Late Bronze Age belong at the latest to the early part of the Middle Period. One of the most interesting finds belonging to the Middle Period is a storage room, in which pithoi were set in a cement floor provided with a system of channels leading to a pithos set below the floor level and obviously intended to prevent loss of the *liquid contents* of the storage pithoi in case of spilling or breakage. When the storage room was used during the period of reoccupation the storage jars were placed on a layer of earth, six inches thick, which had accumulated while the palace was abandoned. When found some of these still contained the remains of their contents, presumably dating from the last period during which the place was occupied—that is, Late Minoan I. Some of the jars held wheat and others lentils. Wheat, likewise presumably of Late Minoan I date, was found elsewhere in the palace. There is no way of knowing what was stored in the room in the Middle Minoan Period; as has been remarked, however, it is plain that at least some of the jars contained liquids— oil or wine; perhaps both. Considerable quantities of household ware

[25]*Eph.* 1912, p. 232.
[26]*Loc. cit.*, p. 163.
[27]*Loc. cit.*, p. 232 and fig. 40.

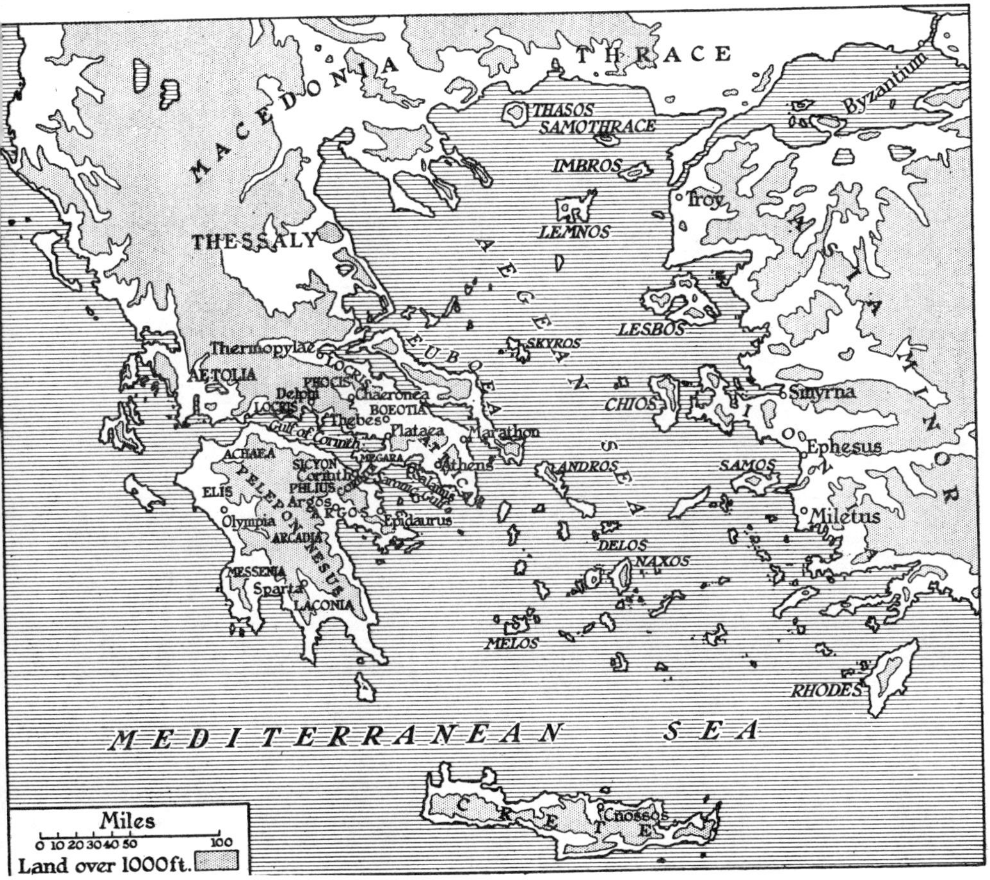
THRACE
MACEDONIA
Byzantium
THASOS
SAMOTHRACE
IMBROS
Troy
LEMNOS
THESSALY
AEGEAN SEA
ASIA MINOR
LESBOS
SKYROS
EUBOEA
Thermopylae
AETOLIA
LOCRIS
PHOCIS
Delphi
Chaeronea
BOEOTIA
Thebes
Plataea
Marathon
Gulf of Corinth
ATTICA
CHIOS
Smyrna
IONIA
Ephesus
ACHAEA
SICYON
MEGARA
Athens
ANDROS
SAMOS
Corinth
PHLIUS
Saronic Gulf
Salamis
ELIS
Argos
ARGOS
Olympia
PELOPONNESUS
Epidaurus
Miletus
ARCADIA
DELOS
NAXOS
MESSENIA
Sparta
LACONIA
MELOS
RHODES
MEDITERRANEAN SEA
CRETE
Cnossos
Miles
0 10 20 30 40 50 100
Land over 1000ft.

were found, mostly of Middle Minoan III date.[28] The only thing suggesting a hearth or a fireplace was a pit against the north wall of room III$_8$ which, it is suggested, since some animal bones were found in it, may have been a hearth where meat was cooked.[29]

One of the most important sites in eastern Crete is Gournià. It was excavated by the American Exploration Society under the direction of Mrs. Harriet Boyd-Hawes.[30] The remains of a considerable town with a small palace were unearthed. Three periods in the development of the town were recognized: an Early Gournià Period corresponding to Middle Minoan III; the Town Period, ending toward the close of Late Minoan I; and a reoccupation period, corresponding to Late Minoan III. This site is remarkable for the amount of evidence it has furnished on the everyday life of the people; Mrs. Hawes observed that the workmen called it a βιομηχανική πόλις.[31] In her work, Gournià, the principal publication of the discoveries there, she devotes Plate I and the accompanying text to the illustration of the types and development of domestic pottery. The only actual remains of food reported are carbonized peas.[32] Animal remains do not seem to have come within the range of the investigation. Among the most interesting of the discoveries are some bronze fish-hooks, barbed and unbarbed, some so large that they must have been used for catching very large fish, perhaps the tunny. The largest one of which the dimensions are given is 9.5 cm. long; the smallest, 2.6 cm. long. Some seal-stones, inscribed tablets, and a considerable amount of painted pottery were also unearthed.

The most important site in the extreme east of Crete is Palaikastro. Among the considerable prehistoric remains found there are a number pertaining to food. One of these is a bowl in the bottom of which about two hundred tiny figurines are moulded in one piece with the bowl. They represent a herd of Cretan short-horned cattle and a herdsman who is described by Glotz[33] as engaged in milking a cow.[34] A smaller bowl was discovered with a single figure of an ox similarly moulded in the bottom, and another with the figure of a dove.[12●] Evans considers the purpose of the bowls votive, and he dates them Middle Minoan I. Many unattached figurines were also found at Palaikastro. Those under consideration are of the pottery type to which the name Kamares was applied, showing that they are of Middle Period date in the strictest sense of the word. Animal figurines[35] were most frequent. Some represent oxen,[36]

---

[28]Mallia I, p. 54.
[29]Ibid., p. 16.
[30]See Gournià.
[31]Ibid.
[32]Ibid., p. 23.
[33]Civ. Eg., p. 191.
[34]But see B.S.A. 8, p. 294.
[35]B.S.A. 9, pp. 376-377, and pl. 13.
[36]Ibid., pl. 13, no. 53.

some rams,[37] swine,[38] dogs,[39] and perhaps hare,[40] and a hedgehog;[41] still others represent the tortoise,[42] and birds.[43] Of the oxen there were two types:[44] a larger type, of which only fragments were found, representing a variety of cattle having slightly curved and twisted horns still common in Crete, and a smaller type with less marked traits. The other animal figurines are of the latter type. The remains of an olive press and a trough (perhaps used for crushing olives), found in a house at Palaikastro, probably also date from the Middle Period.[45] The study of animal remains was not within the purpose of the investigators; they mention, however, the finding of bones of sheep or goats, and the bones and cores of horns of oxen.[46] Wheat and barley, two kinds of peas—the common garden pea and a smaller variety, and olive seeds were also discovered;[47] at Kouramenos, near Palaikastro, was discovered what may be the ruins of an olive press.[48] Another press-bed is described as that of a wine-press.[49] These discoveries are all of Late Minoan date.

In the same part of Crete as Palaikastro are Zakro and Magasà. The former is chiefly noted for the large collection of sealings found there and to which reference will be made.[50] Near Magasà was discovered a Neolithic rock shelter and house, important here principally because of three millstones which were found there. Whereas other Neolithic grinders found in Crete might conceivably have been used for some other purpose than the grinding of grain, these could scarcely have any other use. No food remains were found in the Neolithic house, but the rock shelter contained bones of sheep or of goats, and a few sea shells.[51] A Neolithic cave near Praesos, west of Zakro, yielded only a few sherds.[52]

A considerable quantity of animal remains was discovered in a tholos tomb of Early Minoan I date near Krasì Pediados.[(13*)] The following discoveries are listed: hare (*Lepus creticus* Barett-Hamilton), sheep or goat, swine, hedgehog, dog, and a bored fish vertebra. These remains were examined and identified by Professor Max Hilzheimer of the Märkisches Museum, Berlin. Marinatos comments[53] that the nature of the discoveries led him to believe that the smaller animals were thrown in whole, but that only the heads of the sheep and oxen were put into the tomb. He states that this is the first instance of the discovery of animal bones in a tholos tomb.

---

[37] *Ibid.*, no. 54.
[38] *Ibid.*, no. 57.
[39] *Ibid.*, no. 55.
[40] *Ibid.*, nos. 60 and 63.
[41] *Ibid.*, no. 62.
[42] *Ibid.*, no. 61.
[43] *Ibid.*, no. 59.
[44] *Ibid.*, p. 376.
[45] *Ibid.*, 8, p. 308.

[46] *Ibid.*, p. 314.
[47] *Ibid.*, pp. 280 and 288.
[48] *Ibid.*, p. 334.
[49] *Ibid.*, p. 295.
[50] *J.H.* 22, pp. 76 ff.
[51] *B.S.A.* 11, p. 260.
[52] *Ibid.*, 8, p. 236.
[53] *A.D.* 1929, p. 132.

NOTES

1. Feige (*Petermanns Mitteilungen* 198(1928), p. 63) prefers to qualify the term *Bos primigenius*, used of the Cretan long-horned cattle by C. Keller (*Vierteljahresschrift* 54(1909), pp. 430 ff.), as follows: ". . . Knochenfunde des Urs, oder besser gesagt einer sehr urähnlichen primigenen Rinderrasse. . ." He expressed the opinion that the representations of these cattle in Cretan art regularly represent domesticated cattle, perhaps kept for cult and sporting purposes, and notes the absence of osteological evidence for genuine wild cattle in the South (*Ibid.*, pp. 12 and 63).

Marinatos discusses this subject in connection with some bones of this sort of oxen discovered in an Early Minoan tholos tomb near Krasì Pediatos (*A.D.* 1929, p. 124, note 1). After a careful examination of the bones on which Keller based his opinion, Marinatos states without qualification that all the bones so far discovered in Crete belong to domestic varieties.

2. Evans seems to have considered the study of animal remains to be outside the field of the archaeologist, and for this reason one would not be justified in seeking arguments on the diet or eating habits of the Cretan upper classes from the absence of reports of such remains in his works. On the other hand, the excavators of Phaestos seem to have been fairly systematic in reporting the discovery of animal bones, even when they made no effort to identify them. I have gone over the reports of the excavations there with the intention of noting any similarity in the deposits on that site and in the palaces and houses on the mainland, but I have noted no evidence that the Cretans allowed remains of food to accumulate in their houses as the Mycenaean Greeks seem to have done (Tsountas, *Mycenaean Age*, p. 68; Staïs, *Eph.* 1895, p. 247; Wace, *B.S.A.* 25, pp. 45, 157, 178, 181, 199, and 264; Keramopoulos, *Eph.* 1909, p. 104). The practice of the latter is fully in accord with that of the Homeric Greeks, but hardly consistent with the other habits of a people who made such efforts to achieve cleanliness as the Minoan Cretans made. It seems scarcely credible that the Mycenaeans could have been Cretans and not half-civilized barbarians, if the accumulations in their palaces did really originate as they seem to have. It is true that insufficient evidence has been published to justify a positive conclusion in the matter, but it certainly should help in deciding the ethnic character of the Mycenaeans if it could be established: 1) whether the deposits of bones and the like at Mycenae and elsewhere on the mainland were formed by accumulation of garbage in the house, and 2) whether the Cretan palaces offer parallels. It will be noted that some of these deposits in Mycenae and elsewhere are earlier than Late Minoan III.

3. For an account of the Neolithic finds at Knossos see *P. of M.* 1, pp. 32-55; 2, pp. 10-21; *B.S.A.* 6, p. 17; and C. Keller, *Vierteljahresschrift* 54(1909), p. 430.

4. The excavations at the Zapher Papoura cemetery and at the Isopata tomb are published in *Archaeologia* 59²(1905), pp. 393 ff. This article has also been published in book form, *The Prehistoric Tombs of Knossos*, London, 1906. On the Tomb of the Double Axes and the nearby tombs see *Archaeologia* 65(1914), pp. 1 ff. The excavations at the Maurospelio cemetery are published in *B.S.A.* 28, pp. 243 ff.

5. That this cave is not properly to be called the Dicte Cave is pointed out by Beloch (*Klio* 11, pp. 433 ff.), who accepts it, however, as Hesiod's birthplace of Zeus (*Theogony* 11, 480-484), and the mountain as Ptolemy's ἱερὸν ὄρος (III, 15, 3).

6. The results of these excavations and those at Hagia Triada were published in a series of articles in the *Rendiconti della Reale Accademia dei Lincei*, vols. 12-14 and 19; in *Monumenti Antichi* 12-14 and 19; and in *Memorie del Reale Istituto Lombardo (Classe di lettere, scienze morali e storiche)*, vol. 21, pp. 244 ff. For a more complete bibliography, including the preliminary investigations and covering the material up to 1914, see Fimmen, *Die Kretisch-mykenische Kultur*, pp. 22-23. Note also the publication of the seals and sealings from Hagia Triada, with some from Zacro, in the *Annuario della Scuola Italiana di Atene*, 8(1929), pp. 71 ff.

7. On the discoveries at Phaestos see *M.A.* 12-14 and 19, and *R.A.L.* 10-14 and 16. For a list of the varieties of animals represented in the prehistoric remains at Phaestos, see *Neue Denkschriften* 46(1911), p. 144.

8. On the tholos tomb at Hagia Triada see *R.A.L.* 14(1905), pp. 391 ff.; *Memorie r. Ist. Lomb.* 21(1904), pp. 248 ff.; *Annuario della Scuola Italiana di Atene* 8(1929), pp. 71 ff.

9. In regard to the dating of pictorial seals cf. Evans (*P. of M.* 1, p. 95).

10. It was excavated by Hatzidakis, and the results were published in the *Ephemeris Archaeologike* (1912, pp. 197 ff.), and, summarily, in *Neue Denkschriften* 46 (1911), pp. 160 ff.

11. The excavation of Mallia and the publication of the discoveries is not yet complete. The work was begun by Hatzidakis in 1915, and the results of his work were reported in *A.D.* 1915 and 1919. Among his discoveries were some bone objects made of rib or ankle bones of goats and cattle. The thorough excavation was begun by the French after the World War, and the results have been partly published in *Mallia* 1. Mention should also be made of a Late Minoan tomb east of Mallia, in which some clay larnakes bearing painted animal designs were found. The investigation of this tomb has been reported by Xanthoudides in *A.D.* (6, pp. 154 ff.).

12. On the larger bowl with the herd of cattle and on the dove bowl see *B.S.A.* 8, p. 294; for all three see *P. of M.* 1, pp. 180-181, and fig. 130.

13. See the article by Sp. Marinatos in *A.D.* 1929, pp. 102 ff.; a list of the animal remains is given on p. 124.

III

ARCHAEOLOGICAL EVIDENCE: THE CYCLADES

Attention was first attracted to the prehistoric age of the Cyclades by the discovery on the islands of then unfamiliar pottery and female figurines. Some papers of considerable length had already been written on the subject previous to 1890. Then, in the closing years of the century, the British Archaeological School at Athens carried out important excavations on the island of Melos. On the site called Phylakopi stratified remains were discovered representing the periods since named Early, Middle, and Late Cycladic; prehistoric deposits were also disclosed elsewhere on the island. At about the same time Chr. Tsountas did some excavating and investigating in Paros, Antiparos, Siphnos, Syros, Amorgos, and Despotiko. He investigated some sites of habitations, but the greater part of his discoveries were in cemeteries belonging to the Early Period. During the first ten years of the present century Klon Stephanos studied the Cycladic remains on the island of Naxos. German archaeologists have excavated an acropolis settlement in Paros, a site which was occupied during the Early Period and the early part of the Middle Period, abandoned, and then reoccupied toward the close of the Late Period.[1*]

Although Melos is one of the most important of the Cyclades to the student of general Aegean antiquities, very few discoveries aiding in the study of food have been reported from it; among these few should be mentioned a fragment of a figurine of a cow of Middle Cycladic date; an undated boar's tooth; an undated barbless fish-hook 2.8 cm. long; domestic pottery; and the shells of edible shellfish. Like most of the islands, Melos was first occupied in the Early Cycladic Age; unlike most of them, its importance persisted into the last period of the Bronze Age. Its early importance must have been due to some extent to its monopoly of obsidian, the wide distribution of which over the Aegean world gives an indication of the extent of trade by sea in the Early Age.[1] Its central position aided it to maintain its commercial importance. On the island of Amorgos, Tsountas found three deposits of Early Cycladic date, one of which contained bones of animals, for the most part unidentified, but including the bones of sheep and goats, the jaw of a dog or a fox, and sea shells, mostly limpets. The second contained only sherds and limpet shells; the third contained, besides datable pottery, spindle-whorls, the

---

*Numbers followed by the asterisk and enclosed in parentheses refer to notes at the end of the section; see page 27.
[1]See *Phylakopi*, pp. 216 ff.; cf. *Civ. Eg.*, pp. 35-39.

teeth of sheep or goats, and a few teeth of oxen. The site of a habitation of the island of Paros yielded jaw bones of goats and of sheep; three millstones; some sea shells, including the oyster, the murex, the heart-shell, and the limpet; and some snail shells. Early Cycladic habitations on the acropolis yielded vessels of the sauce-boat type, similar to those found on the mainland. One of these, containing animal bones, seems to have been used as a cooking pot. The graves in Siphnos yielded no objects concerning the subject of food except a *Pecten jacobeus* shell and some crude figurines of birds. Those of Syros contained a jaw and the teeth of sheep; an animal vertebra (unidentified); a considerable variety of shells; fish-hooks; a number of skillet-shaped vessels ornamented on the bottom with pictures of ships having fish at the prow;[2*] a vessel that is probably a lamp; and pottery that makes it possible to date the finds. Habitations on the acropolis yielded rubbers, pithoi, bones of sheep or goats, and limpet shells. Among the shells found in the graves are the murex, *Dentalium elephantinum, Littorina littorea* L., limpet, and oyster. The skillet-shaped objects probably are not cooking utensils at all. They seem rather to be articles of luxury; Tsountas offered the conjecture that they were intended to be filled with water and used as mirrors. Later vessels of similar shape and size, often of bronze, have been found elsewhere. Some of these have been supposed really to be skillets—an explanation of their use which, however, must be taken with caution.[3*]

In one of the graves on the island of Naxos, Stephanos reports the discovery of a small jug (μικρὰ προχοῖς) which contained the remains of olive oil. The jug had in the course of time become filled with earth which, upon removal, was found to smell of rancid olive oil. To make sure of this identification, a specimen was sent to Professor K. Zengeles, of the University of Athens, for analysis. He confirmed Stephanos' opinion.[2] The same grave contained two clay lamps, one of which had three burners and three fuel compartments, connected at the bottom. Other finds made among the rubbish that had been used to level the ground under the floor of a house included spindle-whorls, marble skillet-shaped vessels, and unidentified animal bones.

One of the most important groups of Aegean sites for the study of foodstuffs is that investigated during the 1860's and '70's on the islands of Thera and Therasia. During Middle Minoan III or Late Minoan I a very severe volcanic eruption occurred there and buried considerable settlements under a thick layer of volcanic material.[4*] As at Pompeii and Herculaneum, this resulted in the preservation of the remains of many articles not usually found on sites which continued to be occupied, were abandoned, or met destruction in war. Quantities of grain and whole skeletons of domestic animals have been discovered there; grain

---

[2]*Pr.* 1906, p. 88.

and vegetables in pithoi, barley in feeding pans for the animals, and skeletons of sheep and goats in their stables. In the same deposit a bronze sickle was discovered.[5*] Owing to the circumstances of their preservation, it is possible to affirm confidently that the remains of animals and plant products found under the undisturbed tufa are exactly contemporary, and that they certainly belong to the early part of the Late Bronze Age.[6*] Among domestic animals, sheep and goats are certainly represented. The discovery of a complete skeleton of a goat removes any doubt about there having been goats as well as sheep. In addition, Fouqué discovered bones of horses, asses, and cats in prehistoric context, but not under undisturbed tufa. Hiller von Gaertringen, in a list of animals represented in remains discovered in Thera, names dogs and swine, but he does not state where or by whom they were found. Cattle do not appear to have been represented on any site yet excavated in Thera. Cheese making is suggested by the discovery of numerous conical strainers; a substance, moreover, described as *une matière pâteuse*, found in a house in Therasia, may actually be the remains of cheese. No wheat was discovered; the only grain was barley, but there were large quantities of that.[7*] The olive is the only fruit reported. Olive wood was used in house construction, and an olive press was found in Theresia. The vegetables discovered were lentils, chick peas, and a peculiar variety of peas still grown on the island. Remains of coriander and anise also came to light. Naturally, there were large quantities of sherds, and a considerable amount of whole pottery as well. The pottery has recently been studied and compared with other Aegean pottery.[3]

NOTES

1. For the early researches see J. T. Brent: *Researches among the Cyclades, J.H.* 5(1884), pp. 42 ff.; U. Koehler: *Prähistorisches von den griechischen Inseln, M.A.I.* 9(1884), pp. 156 ff.; and F. Dummler: *Mitteilungen von den griechischen Inseln, M.A.I.* 11(1886), pp. 15 ff. The British excavations in Melos, which began in 1896, are reported in *B.S.A.* 3, pp. 1 ff.; 4, pp. 1 ff.; 17, pp. 1 ff.; and in *Excavations in Phylakopi in Melos*, London, 1904. Tsountas' researches are reported in *Eph.* 1898, pp. 137 ff., and 1899, pp. 74 ff. Klon Stephanos work in Naxos is reported in *Pr.* 1903, pp. 52 ff.; 1906, pp. 86 ff.; 1908, pp. 114 ff.; 1909, pp. 209 ff.; and 1910, pp. 270 ff. The German excavations of the acropolis in Paros are reported in *M.A.I.* 1917, pp. 1 ff. by O. Rubensohn. For a fuller list of excavations in the Cyclades and bibliography to 1914, see Fimmen, *Die Kretisch-mykenische Kultur*, pp. 13 ff. For the Euboean tombs, see Papavasileios, Περὶ τῶν ἐν Εὐβοίᾳ ἀρχαίων τάφων Athens, 1910.

3 L. Renaudin, *B.C.H.* 1922. pp. 113-159.

2. These have been incorrectly stated to have been found in Siphnos (*P. of M.* 2, p. 241, note 1). One object of the same shape was found in Siphnos, but it had no ship design. The error is repeated in Hall, *Bronze Age*, p. 34. Cf. Tsountas, *loc. cit.*, p. 89: τὸ ον ναντίον, ὅσον γνωρίζω, τὰ τηγανοειδὴ σκεύη, ἐὰν ἐξαιρέσωμεν τὸ ἐν τάφῳ 143 τῆς Σίφνου ἀνακαλυφθὲν τεμάχιον . . . μόνον ἐκ Σύρου εἶναι γνωστά . . ." Several objects of the same type were discovered in the tombs in Euboea.

3. May these vessels not be a form of the type of vessel illustrated in *P. of M.* 2, p. 631, fig. 395, lower row, and on the clay tablet, *ibid.* p. 633, fig. 397, lower object to right? Sp. Marinatos interprets these bronze basins as χέρνιβα (*B.C.H.* 53, pp. 365 ff.).

4. For the date see the article *Thera* by Karo in *R.V.G.*, and L. Renaudin, *B.C.H.* 1922, p. 144.

5. For illustration see Perrot et Chipiez, *Histoire de l'Art*, 6, pp. 149-150. The object is described as a saw, but it looks like a sickle, and it is so interpreted by R. C. Bosanquet (*Phylakopi*, p. 224). The original publication was in the *Bulletin de l'Ecole française d'Athènes*, 1870, p. 202.

6. In 1870 Gorceix and Mamêt, of the French School at Athens, excavated some houses near Akrotiri (*Bulletin de l'Ecole française d'Athènes*, 1870, pp. 183 ff.). The results of all these excavations were published by M. Fouqué in Chapter III of his large work *Santorin et ses Eruptions*. In 1899, Robert Zahn excavated a site on the Kamara River, but the results seem never to have been published. A very brief summary is given in Hiller von Gaertringen's *Thera* (III, pp. 39-40).

7. Gorceix and Mamêt reported (*Bulletin de l'Ecole française d'Athènes*, 1870, p. 201) that the grain was wheat or rye, but Fouqué, after careful investigation, was convinced that the only grain discovered on the island was barley (*Santorin*, p. 128).

IV

MAINLAND GREECE AND THE NEIGHBORING ISLANDS, MACEDONIA, AND THE TROAD

The most famous Bronze Age site on the mainland of Greece is Mycenae, in Argolis.[1*] A very considerable amount of food remains has been reported from Mycenae, including wheat; barley; vetch; olive seeds; bones of sheep, goats, swine, and cattle; and sea shells, including oysters and mussels. It is of Late Helladic date. Bones of dogs and horses were also discovered, but not in such quantities as to suggest the use of these animals for food.[2*] Much of the grain and vegetable seeds was found stored in rough pottery jars of a sort now used for the same purpose in that part of Greece, and known as Kotselles.[1] There is also evidence that wheat was stored in leaden jars, for partially melted fragments were found with remains of grain still sticking to them.[2] Considerable quantities of gems and signets furnish pictorial representations of domestic and wild animals. Some other forms of art from Mycenae are of some importance for the study of food—gold ornaments, metal-inlay work, figurines, and the like. Much interest also attaches to the large hearth of the palace, a very large and splendid example of the type known from Late Helladic remains of houses.[3]

Another important site is Tiryns.[3*] The only physical remains of food discovered there are grape seeds; these, however, are of great significance, for they were found in considerable quantity, and were pronounced grape seeds by a botanist, Professor Wittmack of Berlin.[4] Some domestic utensils are reported, but, apart from the grape seeds, the most important objects found at Tiryns are fresco fragments which permit the restoration of two large scenes. One of these represents a boar hunt. A restored scene based on the fragments and reproduced in a colored plate[5] shows two women riding in a chariot through a wood, the trees of which are too conventional to be identified. Another scene showing dogs attacking a boar can also be largely restored. The boar is shown pierced with several arrows and a spear still held in the hand of a man. Another group of fragments shows a boar caught in a net; others show the horns of a deer, and perhaps the body of a hare; still others show men and women leading dogs. The above fragments are all believed to belong to one painting. It is interesting to note that some of the dogs are greyhounds of the Cretan type.[6] While it is true that the

---

*Numbers followed by the asterisk and enclosed in parentheses refer to notes at the end of the section; see page 41.

[1]*B.S.A.* 25, p. 49.
[2]*Pr.* 1886, pp. 75-76.
[3]*Loc. cit.,* p. 67 and pl. 5; Blegen, Korakou, pp. 85 ff.

[4]See Schliemann, *Tiryns,* p. 83.
[5]*Tiryns* 2, pl. 12.
[6]*Op. cit.,* p. 115.

picture is probably the work of a Cretan artist, and is certainly in the Cretan tradition, it must have represented scenes known to the lords of Tiryns. It may be considered, then, illustrative of Greek and Cretan hunting customs in the Late Bronze Age. It proves (1) that large, organized hunts were conducted; (2) that those who took part in them were aristocrats (cf. the use of the chariot and horse, and the dress of the women in the chariot); (3) that women as well as men engaged in hunting; (4) that they used dogs, spears, bows and arrows, and nets; and (5) that boar, deer, and probably hare were worthy to be hunted. Nearly all these facts can be determined from other data, but this painting gives them a coherence and convincing character that no other monument of Aegean antiquity provides.

Another group of fresco fragments shows a herd of deer, identified as fallow deer by the shape of the horns, and therefore as the work of Cretan artists or artists trained in Cretan traditions. This painting is not so significant for us as the other one; it does, however, show the interest of patrons of art in wild life and hunting, and also the familiarity of Cretan artists with deer, a fact which supports the contention that the island was more heavily wooded in Minoan times than it is today. Other fresco fragments show cattle, birds, and the like.

It will be sufficient merely to mention a Mycenaean grave near the Argive Heraeum excavated by Stamatakes.[7]

Because of the detail in the publication, Zygouries is one of the most important Late Helladic sites for the study of pottery.[4a] Remains of many Late Helladic houses were discovered on the site of Korakou on the isthmus of Corinth, the other notable town excavated by Blegen.[8] This site is very important for the study of Late Helladic pottery—in fact the Korakou pottery was fundamental in establishing the Helladic pottery series for, although the finds significant in the study of food are late, the site was occupied from Early Helladic times. The fixed hearths found in the houses provide homely counterparts to the great hearth in the palace at Mycenae. One of these, whose shape permits a statement of dimensions, is roughly square, and measures 1.36 x 1.37 metres (House P). Like the Thessalian hearths (see below), it is made of clay mixed with pebbles and potsherds. Among the figurines some fragments, apparently representing the tails of fish,[9] are significant, because of their Late Helladic date, in the question of whether or not the people of the so-called Heroic Age used fish.

Returning to Argolis, we find a Late Helladic cemetery at Deiras, excavated by Vollgraff,[10] and sites at Asine and Dendra, excavated by

[7]M.A.I. 3(1878), pp. 271 ff.
[8]Korakou.
[9]Ibid., p. 109.
[10]B.C.H. 1904, pp. 364 ff.

Swedish archaeologists. Some animal bones were found in a tomb at Deiras, but they were not identified. Among the objects of art the most significant is a hydria with a painted design representing a goose or a duck, tentatively identified as a *Chenalopex aegypticus*, or Egyptian goose. The fact that Cretan and Mycenaean artists used some purely Egyptian motives must, however, make one hesitant to lean too heavily on artistic evidence in matters of this kind when, as in this case, the picture in question is not a part of a scene that proves its Aegean character.[5*]

The reports of the excavations at Asine[6*] furnish very little material usable in the study of food. Mention is frequently made of the discovery of animal bones but, except for some boar's tusks, no attempt was made to identify them. Among the works of art the most interesting piece is a figure of a duck's head, partly colored, which had probably been attached to the staff of a cane. The tomb at Dendra, also excavated by the Swedes,[11] yielded a considerable quantity of animal bones, representing cattle, sheep, and oxen; boar's tusks; and some fine works of art, including metal vessels and seal-stones. Among the latter is a gold disk, ornamented with octopus designs and comparable to some of the gold vessels from Mycenae and Vapheio.[12]

The so-called Tomb of Vapheio is a collapsed tholos tomb lying a short distance from Sparta, excavated by Tsountas,[13] and chiefly famous for the two gold cups which, having been placed with other funeral furniture in a pit under the floor, are still in good condition. The cups are now generally recognized to be of Cretan workmanship and fully in the Cretan tradition; since they were discovered before anything was known of Minoan civilization, they were long a subject of controversy, and it was even seriously maintained that they were specimens of Phoenician art.[7*] Both of the cups represent the typical long-horned cattle common in Cretan art. On one of them, men are shown in the act of capturing bulls.[14] Evans expressed the view that the scene represents a park rather than wild country because of the presence of palm trees.[15] This adds plausibility to the proposition that the bulls are domestic or, at least, captive bulls. Tsountas, in his original discussion of the cups, raised the question of whether or not the bulls are intended to be wild. He was inclined to think that they were, but he pointed out the fact that the men are unarmed as evidence to the contrary. The use of the net in capturing bulls presents an analogy to the methods of boar hunting described above. In any case, however, I see nothing in the scenes

---

[11]*Art and Archaeology*, 25(1928), pp. 277 ff.; A. Perrson, *Kungagraven i Dendra;* and *A.R.W.* 27(1929), pp. 385 ff.
[12]Perrson, *Kungagraven i Dendra*, colored plate facing p. 76.
[13]*Eph.* 1889, pp. 129 ff., and pls. 7, 8, 9, and 10.
[14]On the identification of the animals as the *Bos primigenius* see C. Keller, *Vierteljahres-schrift*, 54(1909), p. 31.
[15]*P. of M.* 3, p. 177; J.H. 45 (1925), p. 29.

proving that the cattle are wild, and much in the second scene suggesting that they are not, in as much as they are grazing. The only unpeaceful element is that of a man fastening a rope to the hind leg of a bull—a bull which is not struggling. Such performances as bull fights and rodeos in modern times show fully as much violence as the scene on the first cup or other bull-throwing scenes from Cretan art. The olive trees and the palm trees may now be identified with confidence. The doubts formerly raised were due to lack of understanding of Aegean civilization; the representation of the olive tree is now well known from other examples.[16] The other discoveries in the tomb need only brief mention. Most important is a large collection of gems.[17] Among the other finds there is a flying-fish inlay cut out of sheet gold.[18]

Further evidence of the use of grapes in making wine is furnished by a discovery made by British archaeologists near Sparta.[19] This is a sealing from the mouth of a jar, consisting of a potsherd and clay. The sherd had been rounded off and placed in the mouth of a jar; it had then been covered with leaves, over which clay was pressed in, with the result that the clay bears the impress of the leaves. R. M. Dawkins says in his report that these almost certainly were grape leaves. The pottery found on the site is dated in the report as Late Minoan III.

At the site identified by Dörpfeld as the Homeric Pylos (Kakovatos), he excavated some remains of houses and tholos tombs. Among the physical remains of food reported was a quantity of figs,[20] in regard to which Dörpfeld notes the fallacy of arguing the greater age of the *Iliad* as compared with the *Odyssey* from the mention of figs only in the latter. There were also some animal bones in one of the tholoi,[21] which are described as being chiefly of the larger animals. Considerable quantities of painted pottery were collected at Kakovatos, but none of the works of art needs special discussion here.

At Nemea some Early Helladic houses of the later period were discovered by Blegen.[22] In the Early Helladic houses nine saddle querns and some pithoi were unearthed. Near the town was discovered a Neolithic deposit in a cave, which had been used either as a habitation or as a dump for rubbish. In the deposit were found bones of small animals, such as sheep and swine, and one joint large enough to have belonged to a good-sized ox.[23] Another Neolithic deposit discovered near the Argive Heraeum consisted of a mass of black earth containing animal bones and part of the horn of a large bull.[24] Two Neolithic deposits have been found in

[16]Cf. the frescoes at Knossos, *P. of M.* 3, pp. 167 ff., where they are associated with bull-throwing; Evans has pointed out the close analogy to the Vapheio cups.

[17]*Eph.* 1889, pl. 10 and pp. 163 ff.

[18]For its identification as a flying fish, see Marinatos in *Essays in Aegean Archaeology*, pp. 63 ff., and *P. of M.* 3, p. 127 including note 2.

[19]*B.S.A.* 16, pp. 9-10.

[20]*M.A.I.* 32, p. XIV.

[21]*Ibid.*, 34, p. 325.

[22]*A.J.A.* 42(1927), pp. 436 ff.

[23]*Loc. cit.*, p. 439.

[24]Blegen, *A.J.A.* 1925, p. 418.

Corinthia; one at Corinth and the other at Gonià. So far very few Neo-lithic stations have been found in southern mainland Greece.[25]

The site of Orchomenos in Boeotia was inhabited in Neolithic times and into the Late Helladic Age.[8*] The earliest stratum, characterized by the round dwellings, belongs to the Neolithic Period. Bulle[26] gives a detailed description of the floor of these structures, which, as he spe-cifically states, contained no deposit of accumulated household débris ("Die Erde ist ohne Wohnschichten, nur mit vereinzelten Scherben-stückchen durchsetz"). The layer called the *Bothrosschicht* is the Early Helladic layer. The stratum has been named from one of its more notable features, the *bothros*, a pit in the floor of the house, usually lined with clay, containing ashes and sometimes animal bones. Bulle recognized two layers in the remains of this period. More of the bothroi belonged to the second of these than to the first. The earlier bothroi were simply pits; the later ones were lined with clay. Their purpose cannot be de-termined; the possibility that they could have been used as hearths is denied by Bulle himself, since no trace of fire is seen on the walls. Another argument against their use for fire or cooking in hot ashes is the fact that such use would have disturbed the ashes, whereas actually these were found in layers, as though from gradual accumulation.[9*] The animal bones found in the bothroi (none were found in those of the earlier layer) represent the smaller animals—Bulle suggests sheep and goats. In the Middle Helladic stratum considerable remains of grain came to light.[27] They were examined and identified by L. Wittmack of Berlin. The following plant products were represented: barley (*Hordeum*); wheat (*Triticum*); broad beans (*Vicia faba*); vetch (*Lathyrus sativus*); *Ervum ervilia*; a single oat grain; and grape seed discovered in connection with a pithos. In the same layer, some animal bones were discovered, one of which is described as the lower jaw bone of a horse or of a cow. Orchomenos must have been important during the Late Helladic Period, but the remains were badly disturbed by later structures. No discoveries immediately concerning food have been reported.

A number of sites chiefly significant for the study of the Neolithic culture of Greece have been excavated near Orchomenos. A mound near Chaeroneia is made up of several layers of Neolithic remains separated by layers of ashes, with an enclosure of wattles and clay, outside of which earth was heaped. This earth contained bones, but no distinctly marked débris of habitation.[10*] Soteriades maintained that the mound was a place where the dead were cremated with their funeral furniture, whereas

[25] See Mylonas, pp. 80-87.
[26] *Orchomenos*, pp. 23 f.
[27] *Ibid.*, pp. 60-61.

Wace and Thompson assert that it is a site of successive habitations destroyed by fire[28]; in any case, the large quantities of bones and teeth of domestic animals—bones of goats, sheep, and cattle, and teeth of swine or wild boars must, except for a few such things as the skulls of dogs, be the remains of food.[11*] A mound west of Drachmani, appearing to be similar, and containing animal bones—not identified—has been dug into but not thoroughly excavated. It is not too much to suppose that the animal remains are of the same sort as those from the other mound. Remains found at Hagia Marina are certainly those of a settlement. Stratified earth represents almost continuous human occupation from Neolithic to Late Helladic III times with, however, a complete cultural break at the end of the former and of the Early Helladic Period. In the Neolithic layer were found "des os de boeufs ou de chèvres, des cornes de boeufs, de cerfs, des dents de porcs ou, plus probablement, de sangliers, de frêles os de volatiles."[12*] Finds of jars containing grain and dried leguminous vegetables are also reported, but these appear to belong to a later level. Lianokladi, a considerable distance northwest of Drachmani, has much in common with the Thessalian sites, but it was one of the outposts of Early Helladic culture. The Neolithic settlement at Lianokladi was decidedly poorer than the better ones in the North, such as Sesklo and Rachmani. It showed no remains of buildings and, so far as we can gather from the report, no remains of food. The absence of any mention of food in the report can probably be accepted as evidence that no remains of grain, fruit, or nuts were found, for Wace and Thompson speak of such finds on several occasions. It does not seem possible that there could have been no animal remains but, as is frequently the case, the investigators seem to have considered the animal remains so uniform in character as to need no special mention.

Among the sites in Boeotia, Thebes is very important.[13*] The excavators gave considerable attention to the remains of foodstuffs. The reports name sheep, swine, cattle, wild boars, and probably hare as having been found on the site of the so-called House of Cadmus in Thebes; among the sea shells they name the pinna and the pecten—shells regarded as the remains of food. Attention is called to the fact that some of the bones are burnt on the ends, as happens when meat is roasted on the spit,[29] whereas other bones show no signs of such burning. They also comment on the quantities of bones and the like in the floor deposits, noting that the quantity is too great to represent food on hand at the time the building was destroyed, and that it can be explained only by supposing that the people allowed such rubbish to accumulate on floors in the house.[30] Another notable find was the vertebra

---

[28]*P.T.*, p. 197.   [29]*Eph.* 1909, p. 105.   [30]*Loc. cit.*, p. 105.

of a fish. Both this and a fish-hook which was discovered in one of the tombs was found in undisturbed Late Mycenaean, *i.e.* Late Helladic III, context, as Keramopoullos states that he took special pains to determine.[14*] He uses these two finds as a basis of his argument, in his article on the eating of fish, that fish were eaten in Late Mycenaean times. Some bird bones were also discovered in a vessel in one of the tombs,[31] and, in another grave, shells of goose eggs were found. Keramopoullos asserts that he finally decided that these were shells of goose eggs only after examining them carefully, noting the thickness of the shell. He is convinced that the discovery of egg shells in a tomb is evidence that eggs were eaten, and that the various explanations of the presence of eggs in the tombs presuppose their use as food.[32]

The discoveries of art at Thebes need no discussion here beyond a mention of the fact that they included seal-stones and painted pottery.

Aulis yielded some remains of the Early Helladic Period,[33] none of which, however, relate to food; and some graves have been excavated in Chalcis, Euboea, containing pottery similar to the Early Cycladic pottery of Syros, including a large number of skillet-shaped vessels similar to those found on the latter site. The presence of obsidian flakes in some of the graves shows the existence of trade with Melos. No food remains were discovered in these early graves. Some much later graves, however, described as Mycenaean, contained remains of oxen, sheep, goats, and swine.

A tomb at Spata in Attica and the finds made in it of Late Helladic date are described in an article by Haussoulier.[34] Some boar's tusks and some imitation tusks of glass paste were discovered and, in addition, some ivory plaques with representations of wild and domestic animals. The collection of gold objects from Aegina and some house remains there, excavated by Staïs,[35] have already been mentioned. In connection with the latter, bones of animals and birds were discovered forming a floor deposit which caused Staïs to comment on the untidiness of Mycenaean housekeeping.[36] Some Neolithic remains, not yet adequately reported, have been discovered at Athens,[37] as well as some remains of the Early Helladic Period.[38]

One of the most important Thessalian sites is Sesklo.[15*] As in most centers in Thessaly, culture was most flourishing there in the second part of the Neolithic Age. Sesklo was a fortified town on a hill, with a notable architectural development. Tsountas described in considerable detail the fixed hearths and the structures which he regarded as ovens, of which

[31]*Eph.* 1910, p. 207.
[32]*A.D.* 4, pp. 99-100.
[33]*Korakou*, pp. 110 ff.

[34]*B.C.H.* 1878, pp. 203 ff.
[35]*Eph.* 1895, pp. 235 ff.
[36]*Loc. cit.*, p. 247.

[37]See *J.H.* 1924, p. 276.
[38]*Korakou*, pp. 110 ff.

he discovered several examples. Pithoi were used at Sesklo only in the later Neolithic Period. Millstones were found on the site, in all probability belonging to the same period. Remains of food, including wheat and probably barley, and bitter almonds were discovered in undisturbed Neolithic context. The domestication of sheep is attested by the presence of textile tools—spindle-whorls and spools—likewise in undisturbed Neolithic context. Little attention was paid by the excavator to animal remains not in the form of bone tools. Much pottery was found; this is copiously illustrated in Tsountas's work and, to some extent, in Wace and Thompson.

Dimini is a hill-top citadel near Sesklo, which it resembles in many ways. It does not seem to have been settled so early as the latter, but the Second Neolithic Period and later periods are represented there by similar stratification. Similar finds of hearths, ovens, pithoi, other pottery of various sorts, and the like, are reported. As at Sesklo, remains of wheat, barley, and bitter almonds have been discovered and, in addition to these, a fig. A disturbed deposit, belonging to the second or third period, or both, yielded remains of the wild pear and a quantity of figs.[39] In the floor of two of the houses, pits, probably sockets for columns, were found to contain animal bones, in one case identified as those of sheep and goats.[40] Tsountas suggests that the bones may be the remains of sacrifices made when the house was built.

A pierced wild boar's tooth was the only object bearing on the subject of food found at the nearby site called Pyrgos.[41] Tsangli, a site a short distance northwest of Sesklo, was partially excavated by Tsountas and Giannopoulos, but the British excavations, reported in Wace and Thompson's work, were the first to reach virgin soil.[42] This site which, on the whole, showed the usual stratification, permitted a somewhat more detailed subdivision of the early strata than was accomplished at Dimini and Sesklo. No mention is made in the report of hearths and ovens, but fragments of pithoi were found in all the strata from the Second Period on; one was even found in an upper stratum of the First Neolithic Period. Among the more interesting finds were strainers, which occurred here in the strata of the Second and all later periods. Millstones, both saddle querns and flat stones, occurred, but no mention is made of their context, or of that of the whorls, spools, and objects of deer-horn found on the site. Although another station known as Rini also probably dates from the Stone Age, the excavations there have not gone deep enough to produce objects earlier than the Third Thessalian Period.[16*] Among the finds are fragments of pithoi and saddle querns.[43] Tsani, some distance

[39]*D.S.*, pp. 360 f.; *P.T.*, pp. 85 ff.   [42]*M.A.I.* 35(1910), pp. 61 ff.; *P.T.*, pp. 86 ff.
[40]*D.S.*, pp. 51-52.   [43]*P.T.*, pp. 130 ff.; *D.S.*, p. 131, note 3.
[41]*P.T.*, p. 85.

west of Tsangli, was excavated by Wace and Thompson in 1909.[44] The Neolithic Period is subdivided into four strata. In the earliest of these a fragment of a millstone was found. In a later stratum, corresponding to the Third or early Fourth Thessalian Period, and hence to the Early Helladic Age, two millstones were found in association with barley. In the same stratum, and also associated with barley, was embedded a deer-horn hammer of a type regarded as a threshing hammer. Terra-cotta whorls were found in all the strata, but those of the Third Thessalian Period and later are of a different shape from the earlier ones; spools also were found in the early strata. Pithoi first occur in the strata of the Second Period; there is no mention of hearths. Zerelia, some distance southwest of Sesklo, shows a similar stratification. It too was excavated by Wace and Thompson, and reports were given.[45] Pithoi occur from the Second Thessalian Period on. The author comments on the agreement of the sites in this matter. Millstones and a needle of deer-horn were found, but their context is not mentioned. Phthiotic Thebes, north of Zerelia, belongs with these sites, but the reports by Arvanitopoulos do not indicate a good stratification.[46] It is commented[47] that a study of the finds, displayed according to stratification at the Volo museum, does not justify any conclusions except by comparison with other sites. The earliest stratum, which seems to belong to the Neolithic proper, yielded terra-cotta whorls and deer-horn hafts and hammers, as did all the other strata.

Rachmani shows the usual Thessalian stratification from Early Neolithic into the Bronze Age, including two strata belonging to the Neolithic Age, a Chalcolithic stratum, and a Bronze Age stratum.[48] Of these, as is usual on Thessalian sites, the Second Neolithic stratum shows the most prosperous culture, having a greater elaboration of pottery types and a considerable development of architecture. The First Period is, however, by no means crude. Pithoi appear only in the Third Period at Rachmani. The usual Thessalian fixed hearth occurs from the later Neolithic Period on. It is stated in the report that saddle querns were found, but not whether any were found in Neolithic levels. All remains of food belong to the Chalcolithic level. Although no mention is made of them, some remains of animals may have been discovered; the bone and horn tools which are mentioned are post-Neolithic. Marmariani, east of Rachmani, yielded remains of the Iron Age and of the Late Bronze Age, and a few of earlier periods.[49] Of some interest is a deer-horn hammer discovered

---

[44]See report of excavations in *Liverpool Annals*, 1909, pp. 152 ff.; also *P.T.*, pp. 135 ff.
[45]*Loc. cit.*, pp. 118 ff.; *P.T.*, pp. 150 ff.
[46]*Pr.* 1907, pp. 66 ff.; *ibid.*, 1908, pp. 163 ff.; *P.T.*, pp. 166 ff.
[47]*P.T.*, pp. 166 ff.
[48]*Ibid.*, pp. 25 ff.; the original publication of the excavations.
[49]*Ibid.*, pp. 53 f.; *D.S.*, pp. 121 f. and pls. 45-47; *ibid.*, pp. 355-358; *B.S.A.* 31, pp. 1-55.

in association with unthreshed grain. Neither Argissa nor Mesiani Magoula have been excavated. In the mound on the former site, of which a cross-section had been exposed by the waters of the Peneus, Tsountas reported the finding of sherds, largely Neolithic;[50] at Mesiani, he sunk a pit into the side of the slope but learned nothing definite.[51]

A considerable Neolithic deposit has been discovered in a cave on the island of Leukas.[52] Especially noteworthy among the discoveries in this cave are large quantities of bones of the domestic hog. There were also found bones of a small variety of ox and of a sheep similar to the moufflon of Asia Minor—a fact which, the investigator declares, points to a land connection with Asia Minor in late geologic times. A fish vertebra, said to be of a *Carcharias glaucus,* was also discovered in the deposit. Dörpfeld discovered some Early Helladic graves at Nidri, Leukas, which he classed among the *Grabanlagen der achäischer Zeit* (*II. Jahrtausend*). Following the more usual system of chronology Karo asserts that these graves are to be dated by their pottery as Early Helladic. Among the burnt remains were recognized bones and teeth of swine and, in one case, a boar's tooth.

Olynthus in Chalcidice had a Neolithic culture closely related to that of Thessaly; especially to the Second Period of its southeastern branch. The settlement began at a stage slightly earlier than the beginning of the Second Thessalian Period, and ended before the beginning of the Age of Metals; thus the two later Thessalian periods are not represented. Three strata are sharply divided off by layers of ashes.[53] Bones of sheep and oxen and textile implements give evidence of the raising of domestic animals. Actual remains of wheat, figs, and millet, and shellfish were also discovered. Among the ceramic remains were jars, jugs, pots, spit-rests, bowls, and cups. A number of wild boar's tusks show that the Neolithic Olynthians engaged in hunting. Hagios Mamas, west of Olynthus, shows stratification from Neolithic times into the Middle Bronze Age, with a complete cultural break at the end of the former. In the Neolithic level were found bones of sheep or goats; in the Early Macedonian level (ceramic remains definitely connect the site with Macedonia) there were bones of oxen, sheep and goats, and deer; and in the Middle Macedonian level there were bones of oxen and swine. Shells of edible mollusks were also found.[54] Near Olynthus, a little to the north, is Molyvopyrgo, a site occupied in the Early and Middle Macedonian periods.[55] In the Early Macedonian stratum was a bothros which, the excavators assert, was used as an oven.[56] The animal remains represent

---

[50]*D.S.,* pp. 7 ff.
[51]*P.T.;* pp. 54 ff.
[52]G. Velde, *Z. für E.* 1912, pp. 845 ff.; 1913, pp. 1157 ff.
[53]See Mylonas, *Olynthus,* and especially conclusions on cultural relations and chronology on pp. 94-95.
[54]*B.S.A.* 29, p. 156.
[55]*Loc. cit.,* pp. 173 ff.
[56]*Loc. cit.,* p. 173.

sheep, probably goats, hogs, and the ox (probably *Bos longifrons*) in the Early Period; the same type of ox and probably the goat in the Middle Period.

Among the more important Macedonian sites in Macedonia proper is Vardaroftsa in the Vardar valley, inhabited from the Early Macedonian Age into the Iron Age.[57] Discoveries aiding in the study of food include charred grain, pithoi, and strainers; the animal remains[58] represent, for the Early Period, the ox, the goat, the horse, and the elk; for the Middle Period, the ox, the goat, the horse, the dog, the stag (*Cervus elaphus*), the boar, and the tortoise. These remains were examined by Dr. Skouphos of Athens. Vardino, a short distance northwest of Vardaroftsa, was likewise inhabited during the three Macedonian periods. Animal bones, found in all strata, include the sheep, the ox, the pig, and the hedgehog, and, in Stratum IIb, the stag. Clay spindle-whorls were found in strata IIc and III; in Stratum IIb what may be called a hearth was found. The site of Chauchitsa, a short distance north of Vardino, also showed the usual Macedonian stratifications and yielded both animal bones and grain.[59] Kilindir, northeast of Vardaroftsa, yielded similar finds including, among the animal remains identified, the sheep, the goat, the hog, the horse, the dog, the deer, the fox, sea cockles and lake mussels.[60]

The mound of Saratsé,[(17*)] not far from Salonica to the northeast, also contained strata of all periods of the Macedonian Bronze Age and an Iron Age stratum. The discoveries pertaining to food were similar to those made on other Macedonian sites. A round quern appeared in the earliest stratum. Objects, apparently spindle-whorls, appeared in all strata. Spit supports occurred in the strata of the Early and Late Bronze Age. The stratum of the Early Bronze Age yielded remains of ox, pig, sheep or goat, and deer; that of the Middle Age yielded those of pig and sheep or goats, and that of the Late Bronze Age those of pig and, perhaps, the cat. Some specimens of pinna were found in the stratum of the Early Age. No remains of grain are reported. Other sites near Saratsé are Gona and Sedes.[61] In the former mound were found peas (identified by M. Dauphiné of Paris) in the earliest layer, shellfish of all the edible species, animal bones, mostly of the hog, in nearly all the layers,[62] and a hearth.[63] The site of the mound at Sedes was inhabited in Neolithic times, in the Bronze Age, and later;[64] only a few finds, however, in any way relating to food have been reported from the site—articles such as arrowheads, hand mills, spindle-whorls, loom weights, and figurines.[65] Other sites in Macedonia which should be mentioned

[57]W. A. Heurtley, *B.S.A.* 27, pp. 1 ff.; 28, pp. 158 ff.
[58]*B.S.A.* 27, p. 45.
[59]S. Casson, *Archaeologia* 74, pp. 73 ff.
[60]S. Casson, *Antiquaries' Journal* 6(1926), pp. 59 ff.
[61]Léon Rey, *B.C.H.* 40, pp. 257 ff.; 41, pp. 1 ff.

[62]*B.C.H.* 41, p. 245.
[63]*Loc. cit.*, p. 247.
[64]*Loc. cit.*, pp. 154-158.
[65]*Loc. cit.*, 40, pp. 283-284.

for the sake of completeness are Kapoudzilar[66] and Dikili Tash in the Drama Valley, where some Neolithic pottery was discovered.[67]

The early excavations at Hissarlik[18*] yielded extensive quantities of the remains of food, both animal and vegetable; the former in sufficient quantity to permit conclusions on the relative importance of the various domestic animals. Remains of sheep, goats, cattle, and swine were found in the levels belonging to the Early Bronze Period, contemporary with Macedonian A. Virchow concluded on the evidence from the later Early Bronze Age that sheep and goats were much more common than cattle or swine. He did not believe that horses or dogs were eaten, although a few bones of both were discovered. In his report on the remains from the First City he gave a somewhat more prominent place to cattle, and concluded that both cattle and swine were more important in the prehistoric than in the modern Troad. He comments on the much greater quantities of bones of domestic than of wild animals. E. L. Moss stated that the cattle were probably *Bos longifrons*. In the first and second levels were discovered remains of wheat, described as *Triticum durum var. Trojanum,* but none of barley. There were, moreover, hogbeans, peas, and bitter vetch.[19*] No remains of olives were reported, and it is stated that no lamps were found. Of the remains of vertebrate fish, some were identified as belonging to large tunny fish, a sort of shark, and to the ray. In addition the shells of the usual edible mollusks and, among the wild game, remains of wild boar, deer, hare, and a very few bones of wild birds were discovered. Virchow observed that the condition of the bones indicated that the people of prehistoric Hissarlik cooked meat by boiling. The usual mill seems to have been the saddle quern. Other objects of interest discovered on the site of Troy are spoons of ivory and terra-cotta, pieces of terra-cotta that Schliemann believed to be the remains of round table tops, and a copper blade, perhaps that of a sickle, belonging to the Sixth City.

The site of Thermi,[20*] ten kilometres north of Mytelene, has revealed a prehistoric culture related to that of Troy, and dated as contemporary with Troy I and II. Remains were discovered of sheep, cows, pigs, and dogs, and of grain, but the detailed report of these finds has not yet been published.

Among the more interesting finds are the bothroi, similar to those discovered at Orchomenos, discovered in the strata of the second, and early part of the third period of Thermi. Five superimposed towns were discovered, of which the first two belong to the first ceramic period, the third to the second ceramic period, and the fourth and fifth to the third ceramic period; this latter period is related to Troy II.[68] Periods I-II

[66] *Loc. cit.,* 41, pp. 91 ff.   [67] *Loc. cit.,* p. 179.   [68] *B.S.A.* 30, p. 2.

are earlier than Early Helladic; Period III, *e.g.* Town IVa, are contemporary with it.[69] Thus it appears that only the latest of the bothroi are contemporary with the Early Helladic Period, and Miss Lamb therefore concludes that the bothroi furnish further evidence of a movement from Anatolia to Greece at the beginning of the Age of Metals. As to the use of the bothroi, Mr. Hutchinson decided that they are intended as drainage pits, both because of evidence connected with the pits themselves and because similar pits are used for that purpose in modern Lesbian houses.[70] It is to be noted that the bothroi at Thermi contain ashes, stones, and sherds, but rarely bones.

Both simple hearths and bee-hive ovens—one of the latter well preserved—seem to have been common. The former were of the fixed type, built up of clay, pebbles, stone, and sherds. One is described as measuring 1.17 x .81 metres.[71] The bee-hive ovens were, at times at least, built inside the houses. The one which is preserved[72] consists of a dome, 28-30 cm. high, inside measurement, and 64 x 65 cm. wide, resting on a base similar to a hearth. Another similar oven, not so well preserved,[73] seems to have had a fire-box under the floor. Another culinary device consisted of a pithos lying on its side and partly imbedded in the clay of the upper surface of the hearth so that it would be heated by the fire.[74] Another example[75] of the same arrangement differed from the first in the fact that the pithos was flanked with brick and stones, and had a flue at the back.

NOTES

1. Mycenae was excavated by Schliemann, whose book reporting the excavations is dated 1873. Later excavations at Mycenae, both on the acropolis and in the cemeteries, were carried on by Chr. Tsountas, whose reports appeared in *Pr.* (especially 1886, pp. 59 ff.) and in the *Eph.* (especially 1886, pp. 119 ff., and 1891, pp. 1 ff.). In 1893 he published a book in Greek on Mycenae under that name, to which I have not had access; it was, however, revised and published in English (Tsountas and Manatt, *The Mycenaean Age*, 1897). Since the World War the British School at Athens has conducted careful excavations in the Palace, the Grave Circle, and the Bee-Hive Tombs. This work, in addition to its independent value, serves as a check on Schliemann's reports (*B.S.A.* 25, pp. 1 ff.). Karo wrote a study on Mycenae which was to have appeared in 1915 (*M.A.I.* 1915, pp. 113 ff.), but which was not actually published until 1927. This has recently been republished with illustrations of the Mycenaean finds (*Die Schachtgräber von Mykenai*, Munich, 1930). Additional bibliographical material can be found in Fimmen, *Die kretisch-mykenische Kultur*, p. 11.

[69] *Loc. cit.*, 31, p. 150.
[70] *Loc. cit.*, p. 149.
[71] *Loc. cit.*, 30, p. 15.
[72] *Loc. cit.*, p. 16.
[73] *Loc. cit.*
[74] *Loc. cit.*, p. 17.
[75] *Loc. cit.*

2. Here, as at Tylissos, the quantities of animal bones justify some conclusions on the relative importance of the various domestic animals. Tsountas (*Mycenaean Age*, p. 69) says that bones of swine exceeded all others, being about equaled in quantity by those of sheep and goats. Wace, in mentioning the various animals represented in the deposits (*B.S.A.* 25, pp. 157, 178, and 181), states that they are predominantly sheep and swine. It will be remembered that at Tylissos the remains of sheep were the most numerous, being about equaled by those of swine.

3. Tiryns was also early excavated by Schliemann, who published some material on it in the fore part of his work on Mycenae, and a book devoted to it (English edition, 1885) chiefly interesting to the student of architecture, inasmuch as the excavation was largely directed, and a considerable part of the book written, by Dörpfeld. Later excavations have been carried out by the German Institute in Athens, the second part of whose report *(Tiryns)* contains the material bearing on food.

4. See Blegen, *Zygouries,* pp. 5-28, 43 ff., 76 ff., and 180 ff.

5. Vollgraf gives M. G. Schweinfurth as authority for his identification of the bird, but he acknowledges that other naturalists whom he consulted were more skeptical.

6. The Swedish excavations at Asine were directed by C. Frödin and A. Perrson, and the reports were published in French in the *Årberättelse = Bulletin de la Société des Lettres de Lund,* 1921, pp. 17 ff.; 1923, pp. 25 ff.; 1924, pp. 162 ff.; and 1925, pp. 23 ff.

7. Their date is placed as M.M. III to L.M. I (*P. of M.* 3, pp. 177 ff.; Hall, *Bronze Age,* p. 154). They are illustrated in color on plate 9, *Eph.* 1899, and Tsountas' description is given *ibid.* pp. 159 ff.

8. Schliemann did some excavating at Orchomenos; the important work, however, was done by H. Bulle, beginning in 1903, and was reported by him in an extensive work published in the *Abhandlungen der philosophisch-philologischen Klasse der kaiserlichen bayerischen Akademie der Wissenschaften,* vol. 24.

9. Wace and Thompson suggest that they may have been used for baking with hot ashes, a method which, they say, was used by the Klephts, and is known in the South Balkans generally (*P.T.,* p. 195). I am informed by Dr. W. A. Oldfather that it is also very common today in Persia. The excavators of Molyvopyrgo are convinced that a bothros discovered there in the Macedonian A level was used as an oven (*B.S.A.* 29, p. 173). Dr. George Mylonas has studied the subject of prehistoric and modern bothroi, but he has been unable to reach a definite conclusion as to the use of the former. He points out, however, that the close analogies between the ancient bothroi and the modern ones, which are used for cooking, deserve serious consideration ('Η Νεολιθική 'Εποχή ἐν 'Ελλάδι, pp. 161-164). On the other hand, Mr. R. W. Hutchinson has concluded, on the basis of the recent discoveries at Thermi in Lesbos, that bothroi are really drainage pits to keep houses dry in winter, and he mentions modern analogies found in Lesbos (*B.S.A.* 31, p. 149). It is asserted that the bothroi of Thermi are earlier than those of Orchomenos, and that this fact confirms a movement from Anatolia to Greece about the beginning of the Early Helladic Age.

10. *M.A.I.* 1903, pp. 302 ff. (a mention in connection with an account of the battlefield of Chaeroneia); *M.A.I.* 1905, pp. 113 ff. (a description of the Neolithic mound near Chaeroneia, and a discussion of the probable extent of the settlement around Elatea-Drachmani in Neolithic times); *M.A.I.* 1906, pp. 392 ff., and especially beginning on p. 396 (a review of the material about the finds near Chaeroneia and Drachmani); *Eph.* 1908, pp. 63 ff. (a detailed account of the finds at Chaeroneia and Drachmani); *Pr.* 1909, pp. 123 ff.; and *ibid.* 1910, pp. 159 ff. (a brief report on some further work at these sites). *R.E.G.* 25(1912), pp. 252 ff. recapitulates the above material, and reports in some detail the excavations at Hagia Marina. See also *P.T.*, ch. 9, pp. 193 ff.

11. *R.E.G.* 25(1912), p. 264. In *Pr.* 1909, p. 124, he asserts that he had found horse teeth in the mound.

12. *R.E.G.* 25(1912), p. 278. It seems a little odd that he hesitates to say whether there were bones of cattle as well as those of goats, especially when he seems not to hesitate in identifying the bones in the mound at Chaeroneia. It is to be noted that most excavators, when they attempt to identify animal bones, have no hesitation in distinguishing those of cattle from those of sheep or goats, but are very hesitant in distinguishing between the latter. If the distinction is impossible, the remains must be too fragmentary to identify at all. That cattle are represented is proved by the horns.

13. The excavations at Thebes have been conducted by the Greek Archaeological Society, and the results have been published in the *Ephemeris,* the *Archaeologikon Deltion,* and the *Praktika,* by A. Keramopoullos. I have read and excerpted the pertinent parts of the following reports: *Eph.* 1909, pp. 57 ff.; 1910, pp. 209 ff.; *A.D.* 3, pp. 80 ff.; *Pr.* 1922-1924, pp. 28 ff.; 1927, pp. 32 ff., and 1928, pp. 45 ff.

14. On the fish-hook see *A.D.* 3, pp. 177-178, and fig. 129, 1. It measured 4.5 x 1.3 cm. On the fish vertebra see *ibid.* p. 179, and Keramopoullos' article on the eating of fish (*A.D.* 4, pp. 90 ff.). To anticipate the objection that the vertebra might be that of an eel, he had it examined by G. D. Athanasopoulos of the Zoölogical Museum, who decided that, while the exact species could not be determined, it belonged to one of the *Teleostei,* and certainly not to the eel.

15. The most complete account of the excavations is the full report given by Tsountas (*D.S.* 68 ff.), which is summarized by Wace and Thompson (*P.T.*, pp. 58 ff.).

16. On the Thessalian chronology see the introduction and the accounts of the excavations of Sesklo and Dimini in *Prehistoric Thessaly,* pp. 1 ff., 58 ff., and 75 ff.

17. The excavation of the Toumba of Saratsé by the British School at Athens has been reported in the *B.S.A.* 30, pp. 113-150, by W. A. Heurtley.

18. Schliemann began his excavations of the mound of Hissarlik in 1871; Dörpfeld was engaged to aid in the work in 1882. The results of Schliemann's excavations were published in his *Ilios* (English edition, New York, 1880), and *Troja* (English edition, New York, 1884). Further reports on the work were published by W. Dörpfeld (*Troja und Ilion,* Athens, 1902). The animal remains came to the attention of R. Virchow, who spent some time on the site, and of E. L. Moss. Part of Virchow's findings were published in the *Abhandlungen der k.*

Akademie der Wissenschaften zu Berlin (1879), under the title *Beiträge zur Landeskunde der Troas,* but the most complete account of the food remains which he examined is contained in an article published by him in the *Verhandlungen der Berliner Gesellschaft* (1879, pp. 254 ff.). An extensive passage of the latter is quoted by Schliemann (*Ilios,* pp. 314 ff.). A further report by Virchow on some bones belonging to the earliest settlement, collected in the year 1882, is published as an appendix to Schliemann's *Troja* (pp. 348 ff.).

19. The vegetable remains from Troy were submitted for identification to Professor L. Wittmack of Berlin.

20. Thermi is being excavated by the British School at Athens, and reports are appearing in the *Annals.* In the above account the reports by R. W. Hutchinson and W. Lamb have been used (*B.S.A.* 30, pp. 1-52; 31, pp. 148-165).

V

LINGUISTIC EVIDENCE

The study of place names in Asia Minor, Greece, and the Greek islands has demonstrated that at a very early time the same language or group of related languages was spoken in those lands, and it has provided criteria by which many words in the Greek language can be identified as loan words from this language or group of languages. A considerable part of these words are words of civilization. It is very natural that the Greeks should have made such additions to their vocabulary. When they entered the Mediterranean lands they found a fauna and flora in many respects different from that of their old home. They also found an old and complex civilization. Many examples could be given of other peoples adopting vocabulary along with material elements of culture from the people who possessed them earlier. Thus in most European languages the names for American plants and animals, and for man-made objects and institutions peculiar to the Indians, very often have their origins in the various languages of the Western Hemisphere. Examples in English are *tobacco, potato, maize, hominy, tomahawk, wampum, wigwam,* and *powwow.* That the English learned much of their knowledge of navigation from the Dutch and of music from the Italians is shown by the Dutch and Italian elements in the English language. I think it a very fair assumption that, if the Greeks of historic times called a Mediterranean object by a word from the language of the earlier peoples, they learned the use of that object from those peoples or, at least, that they found the object in use among them. One apparent difficulty in applying linguistic evidence in the study of Aegean civilization is the fact that there is the possibility that such words could have entered the language from Asia Minor itself even during historic times. The force of this objection is lessened, however, by the fact that the Aegean area, including Asia Minor, had a common culture from very early times, and that the flora and fauna of the different parts of the whole region are very similar. It can, indeed, be shown that many of the words in question were already in the Homeric language, and that very few entered later.[1*] But the mere fact that a word existed in a language of Asia Minor is evidence for its having once belonged to the language group of the whole Aegean, especially if it applies to a plant or animal widely distributed in the eastern Mediterranean, and in those cases where West Semitic or Latin has the word from a third source independently of Greek, the probability of its being an Aegean word is very great.

---

*Numbers followed by the asterisk and enclosed in parentheses refer to notes at the end of the section; see page 47.

Blegen[1] has recently published a paper in which he seeks to prove that the spread of this language and the place names belonging to it occurred during the Early Bronze Age. If this proposition is accepted, it follows that many of the words later adopted into the Greek language must have been in use in this Early Bronze Age, and that the plants and animals for which the Greeks used such loan words were known to the people of that time. If, on the other hand, we accept the view defended by Matz that the spread took place from the culture area to the northwest of Asia Minor, a still greater antiquity might be assumed for this class of words within the Aegean area. In any case it would not be necessary to accept a later date for them.

Considerable, though by no means exhaustive study has been given to this class of words. A. F. Pott,[2] dealing with the subject of place names, listed a large number ending in -νθ, or containing the intervocalic σ, and he called attention to the distribution of this class of names in Asia Minor. He recognized that they probably belonged to a non-Greek language, perhaps Pelasgian, and that some common nouns have similar endings. He names ἄψινθος, ἴονθος, κήρινθος, μήρινθος, πείρινς, ὑάκινθος, βόλινθος, and βόνασος. He refers to his review of Benfey's *griechisches Wurzelwörterbuch*,[3] in which he called attention to these words and their probable non-Greek etymology. Despite this good beginning, the matter did not get the attention it deserved. Curtius either omitted a word altogether, or sought parallels in other Indo-European languages and, if possible, attempted to give a plausible etymology. The place names seem to have attracted general attention earlier than the common nouns. Pauli[4] and Oberhummer[5] give attention to the question, and August Fick[6] has written what purports to be an exhaustive work on this class of names. It is on the basis of Fick's work that the map to illustrate Blegen's article[7] was prepared by Haley. Kretschmer, in the history of the Greek language referred to above, and Fick both give some attention to vocabulary as well as to place names. In an article on the inscriptions of Praesos, R. S. Conway discusses the subject,[8] and A. Meillet in several of his works has taken up the matter briefly. The most exhaustive treatment of the subject to which I have had access is that of A. Cuny.[9] He classifies the words that he supposes to have their origin in the linguistic group in question into five categories, namely: I, words ending in -νθ; II, words with intervocalic -ς; III, words with initial -σ plus a vowel; IV, words

[1]*A.J.A.* 1928, pp. 146 ff.
[2]*Die Personennamen.*
[3]*Berl. Jahrb.* 1840, p. 630.
[4]*Vorgriechische Inschriften von Lemnos*, 1, pp. 47 ff. (The reference is at second hand from Kretschmer, *Geschichte der griechischen Sprache*, p. 402).
[5]*Akarnien*, p. 57.
[6]*Vorgriechische Ortsnamen.*
[7]*A.J.A.* 1928, pp. 146 ff.
[8]*B.S.A.* 8, pp. 154 ff.
[9]*R.E.G.* 1910, pp. 154 ff.: *Les Mots du Fonds préhellénique du Grec, Latin, et Sémitique occidental.*

existing in Greek and Latin, but not loan words from one to the other; and V, words bearing a similar relation to Greek and West Semitic. E. Meyer considered Cuny frequently overbold,[10] but he agreed with him in principle, and he mentioned in particular several words that both Greek and Semitic probably owed to the ancient language of Asia Minor. Glotz[11] compiled from various sources a list of words of this class. Finally there must be mentioned the latest edition of Boisacq's dictionary[12] which takes into account the possibility of Anatolian-Aegean etymology, but with considerable conservatism, and Leo Meyer's large work on Greek etymology.[20]

NOTES

1. Compare the linguistic character of the following words for things known to have been introduced late: cat (αἴλουρος); chestnuts (κάστανος); chicken (ἀλεκτρυών); cinnamon (κιννάμωμον); melon (πέπων); and pepper (πέπερι).

2. The recent German work which seeks a *Protindogermanisch* element in the language or family of languages to which this class of words belongs in no way invalidates the proposition that such words can be recognized by their structure, for the hypothetical *Protindogermanisch* branched off from the main stock long before the *Urindogermanisch* assumed the form it had when it broke into its eastern and western branches. It rather makes easier the acceptance of words whose apparent connection with Indo-European languages would thus be explained.

[10]*G. des A.* 1², ed. 3, p. 705.   [11]*Civ. Eg.*, p. 441.   [12]*Dict. Etym.*

VI

PLANT PRODUCTS

Virchow,[1] commenting on the remains of food at Troy, asserted that he did not believe the ancient people there to have been meat-eaters, despite the great abundance of animal remains. The likelihood is that grains and vegetables were eaten much more frequently and were depended on much more than animal flesh, especially by the humbler people in the civilized countries. Now, since such folk are more numerous than savages or gentlemen, their main food supply should be discussed first, even if it has left less relics for modern archaeologists to discover. What cereals, vegetables, fruits, and nuts were known to the prehistoric peoples of the Aegean world? How early was each plant known and used in each region? How was it cultivated? How was it prepared for the table? It must be admitted that some of these questions cannot be answered at all, and none of them can be answered fully; archaeological and linguistic study, however, has not been without result, and the material summarized above prevents these conclusions.

Cereal grains, at least wheat and barley, were already known and cultivated in Neolithic times, probably throughout the region. Actual specimens of wheat, Neolithic in date, have been found at Sesklo and at Olynthus; specimens of barley, likewise surely of Neolithic date, have been discovered at Dimini. Neolithic deposits of millet have been unearthed at Olynthus. Due to the fact that no actual remains of grain have been discovered in Cretan Neolithic deposits, or in any Cretan deposits earlier than M.M. III, some authorities have denied that the Neolithic Cretans practiced agriculture. But true millstones of Neolithic date discovered in Crete remove our doubts about the cultivation of grain there in those times, and we are left only to wonder which of the grains known on the mainland were also known to the Cretans.[1*]

Wheat and barley certainly were the principal grains of the Aegean world in the Bronze Age. Samples of millet have been found only in the North, namely, at Marmariani in Thessaly and at Olynthus, where they appeared in the context of the Middle and Late Bronze Age. The French excavators of Thera believed that they had found rye there, but the grain was not, it seems, examined by a botanist. With these exceptions, the only grains discovered are varieties of wheat and barley.[2*]

Cretan and Mycenaean artists, unlike the Egyptians, seldom portrayed farmers at work; the tools, moreover, were frequently not of such

---

*Numbers followed by the asterisk and enclosed in parentheses refer to notes at the end of the section; see page 55.
[1] Z. für E. Ver., 1879, p. 269.

material as to last very long in the rubbish heap, nor were they stored in cities or palaces, where accumulating débris would enable archaeologists to date them. The result is that little can be known, although much can be surmised about the farms, orchards, and gardens of prehistoric Crete and Greece. It has been supposed that, in the Bronze Age in Crete, great manors or plantations were managed by the kings and nobles.[2] The land was plowed with a primitive plow, not unlike that described in Hesiod and still seen in modern Crete, of which a picture forms part of the Cretan hieroglyphic system.[3] The grain was harvested with a sickle, usually of bronze, but at times probably of wood with flint teeth. After having been threshed, the grain was separated from the straw with the winnowing fork.[3*] The inhabitants of prehistoric Thessaly seem to have used a hammer of deer-horn in threshing.[4] Grain was usually stored in stone jars; sometimes, however, it was stored in bins or on the floors of rooms.

To the end of the Bronze Age the Aegean peoples used saddle querns and simple millstones to grind their grain. Just how the meal was used is not clear for, with one exception, no sample of bread has been discovered. This, found at Marmariani in Thessaly, and dating from the Third or Fourth Period of the Thessalian series, is made of millet. Except the people of Thermi and, perhaps, the Thessalians, none of the prehistoric Aegean peoples can be proved to have used ovens. Among the hearth-like structures discovered at Dimini and Sesklo are some with incurving walls which seem to be the remains of a half-dome. The floor is similar to that of a hearth, containing quantities of potsherds, the purpose of which, Tsountas believed, was to hold heat. Some of them were built on a base, but no fire-box was provided under the floor even when there was sufficient space. Of course, a fire-box is not an indispensable part of such an oven. That these structures were used in cooking seems obvious; according to the description it is hard to doubt that they were covered with a half-dome. That they could have been ovens seems plain, and no better explanation of them has been offered, but their significance in the development of Aegean civilization is doubtful for, so far, they are isolated examples. Nevertheless, the reasons given for doubting Tsountas' explanation, unsupported by an alternative explanation, seem insufficient.[4*]

Tsountas anticipated the objection to his theory that bread was unknown until later times, and cited O. Benndorf's article.[5] The argument here is that leavened bread was unknown in Homeric times. Benndorf supported his contention by calling attention to the fact that no ovens or

[2]See Glotz, *Civ. Eg.*, p. 187.
[3]*S.M.*, sign number 27.
[4]*P.T.*, pp. 53-54; *D.S.*, p. 360.
[5]In *Eranos Vindobonensis*, Vienna, 1893, pp. 372 ff.

other equipment for making bread had been discovered at Troy, Mycenae, or Tiryns, and that no words for such things were used in Homer.
Tsountas tried to show that, since ἱπνός is an Indo-European word, ovens
must have been known in Homeric times. However, the etymology of the
word is by no means certain.[6] Granted that the Neolithic peoples of the
Aegean region did not use yeast, there seems to be no reason why they
may not have used ovens to make unleavened bread; that at least some of
the people of the mainland did do so is shown by the specimen of bread
discovered at Marmariani.

Whatever may be the case as to the identity of the structures discovered at Dimini, there can be no doubt about the character of the
ovens discovered at Thermi, for the dome of one of them was discovered
intact (see the discussion of the excavations there, above). These, however, like those of Dimini, have, so far as present knowledge goes, no
counterparts elsewhere. In connection with the objection to regarding
those of Dimini as ovens since they have no fire-box and since they are
located inside houses, it should be noted that those of Thermi, too, usually
lack a fire-box, and were placed inside the house.

Certain pottery covers, suggesting the lid of modern roasters, may
have served as ovens.[7] Bread could be placed on a slab or dish of stone or
pottery ware, covered with a cover of the sort referred to, and placed
over the coals. A similar device is now used by the nomad peoples of
Greece. The bread is placed on a three-legged metal pan, under which a
fire is built, and is covered with a cover of metal insulated with sand.
This method is said to serve its purpose well.[8] Bread could also have been
baked in hot ashes, as some people in Asia Minor, for example, bake their
bread even in modern times.[9] Meal must also have been used in the form
of porridge or mush.

In the last period of the Bronze Age, we may confidently believe, leguminous vegetables, such as beans and peas, were known and used throughout the Aegean region.[5*] In Crete and the Cyclades no discoveries
of this sort of food have been made which can be dated earlier than the
Late Bronze Age.[6*] On the mainland, however, the use of leguminous
vegetables is proved to go back to the beginning of the Age of Metals.
It seems inherently probable that they were known even in Neolithic times
and throughout the Aegean, but proof that this is true can be had only
if, through further excavation in Crete and on the mainland, datable
specimens are found.

Beans, peas, and other similar legumes must have been raised in
gardens much as they are raised today. In season they must have been

[6]See Boisacq, Dict. Etym.
[7]For examples, see Gournià, p. 30. and pl. 2, nos. 34, 39, 40, 41, and 43.
[8]National Geographic Magazine, December, 1930, p. 707.
[9]Benndorf, loc. cit., p. 373; see also note 9, p. 42.

stewed fresh. Lacking the means for preserving the moist vegetable, the men of the Bronze Age—or more probably their women—dried them and kept them in the large pithoi, so common in all Aegean homes, ancient or modern. Then, during the seasons when the garden produced no fresh beans or peas, the dried ones could be ladled out of the pithos, soaked, we may suppose, over night, and stewed for dinner.

Of garden vegetables only dried seeds, such as those of beans, peas, and related plants could survive. For the others we must rely on such scanty evidence as we can get from language. The Greek words for celery, chicory, cucumber, garlic, leek, pumpkin, rampion, and water parsnip, as well as the names for peas and chick peas, seem to have their origin in the pre-Greek language of the Aegean, and hence suggest that the presence and probably the use of the plants go back to the Bronze Age, probably to its beginning.[7*] It must be admitted that, even where a plant was known and named—even native to the country—we do not *know* that its fruit was eaten. For instance, the belief that an edible plant, such as the tomato, is poisonous may long keep people from eating it. But the doubt is not very serious in the case of the plants named above.

The discussion of garden plants will not be complete without the naming of a few usable as condiments. Anise and coriander seeds were found in the ruins on Thera-Therasia,[10] and thus date from the last period of the Bronze Age. Linguistic evidence suggests, if it does not prove, the knowledge and use of calamint, mint, sesame, silphium, and wormwood. The silphium plant, moreover, appears to be represented by a sign in the Cretan hieroglyphic system.[11]

The cultivation of the olive and the use of olive oil dates back, in the southern Aegean at least, to the early part of the Bronze Age. The doubts about the early use of the olive have been removed, for the latter part of the Bronze Age at least, by a series of archaeological discoveries,[12] and the fact is no longer questioned. Since, however, we have no valid reason for assuming that a thing known later was *ipso facto* known earlier as well, archaeological proof of the use of olive oil in the Early Minoan and Early Cycladic periods is well worth presenting. The actual remains of olive oil were found in a jug in an Early Cycladic grave on the island of Naxos.[13] Near this jug were found two objects which may be lamps, one with three chambers, connected at the bottom, perhaps for fuel. This fact in the construction of the lamp, if it is one, indicates the use of liquid fuel. Once it has been established that oil

---

[10]*Santorin*, p. 128; von Gaertringen, *Thera*, p. 40.
[11]*P. of M.* I, pp. 284-285.
[12]Editors' notes to the 1911 edition of Hehn's *Kulturpflanzen und Haustiere*, pp. 118 ff.
[13]*Pr.* 1906, p. 88.

was used in these lamps, it is a fair inference that the presence of lamps anywhere in the culture area of the Aegean proves that olive oil was known and used there. To go a step further and say that olives were cultivated is well justified, especially in view of the fact that an olive press was discovered in the context of the following period, when the olive also appears in art and in the hieroglyphic script. Lamps have been discovered in the Mesarà at Koumasà, Hagia Eirene, Portì, and Christos.[14] Lamps showing marks of flame at the spout or wick-slot were found at all the sites named in the Mesarà, and they date from the Early Period and the early part of the Middle Period—that is, from Early Minoan II at the latest to Middle Minoan I. Although I can cite no examples of lamps from Early Helladic sites, the close relation between them and the Cyclades makes the supposition that olives and oil were known there almost certain.[8*] Schliemann[15] states specifically that no lamps were discovered at Hissarlik.[9*]

Oil was prepared from olives by a method still used in Crete. The fruit is first drenched in hot water, and then crushed in a simple machine; then it is placed in settling vats. After the oil floats on the surface of the water, the latter is drawn off through a spout in the bottom of the vat, and after it the oil. Such vats, made of earthenware, have frequently been discovered, and their use has immediately been recognized by modern Cretans.[16]

We must suppose that the olives themselves were prepared for eating, and that the oil served as a cooking fat and a salad oil, much as it does now in Mediterranean countries. It was stored in pithoi, which, in warehouses such as those of the king of Crete, were sometimes enormous. The size and number of the storage jars proves that great quantities of oil were produced, not only for domestic use, but also for export. Olives must have been the chief income crop of Minoan Crete.

Were wine and vinegar known to the Aegean peoples of the Bronze Age? If so, were they known from early times, or were viticulture and wine-making introduced late? It will scarcely be disputed that wine was common toward the close of the Bronze Age; certainly the Homeric poems assume that it was (cf. Hehn, 1911, p. 65). On the other hand, the use of the wine in Minoan times has not been generally accepted. Evans[17] asserts that the use of a sort of beer seems to have preceded the use of wine in Crete; in another article[18] he says that it is a moot point whether grape wine was known in Minoan Crete, whereas some have either taken it for granted, or have given no reason for their assumption, that wine was used. Thus Burrows[19] and Chapoutier[20] speak of wine,

[14]*Mesarà*, pp. 14, 52, 63, and 71.
[15]*Troja*, p. 145.
[16]See *Gournià*, p. 27, and *B.S.A.* 8, p. 268.
[17]*P. of M.* 1, p. 415.

[18]*J.H.* (1925), p. 19.
[19]*Discoveries in Crete*, p. 91.
[20]*Mallia* 1, p. 10.

and Glotz[21] seems convinced that the Minoan Cretans used wine. He asserts that the common Early Minoan vessels resembling teapots may have been used for pouring wine. This seems quite possible, since they were certainly luxury articles, suitable for table use.[22] They may, indeed, have been used for beer—at least they do not prove the use of wine—but, if Minoan beer-drinking habits in any way resembled modern ones, these pots would have been rather small; their size is much more suitable for filling wine cups.

Only the seed of the grape has any chance of escaping decay well enough to be recognized after so many years, and it is very small. No one should be surprised to learn that grape seeds have not been found frequently, or argue from the absence of such seeds at any place or time that wine was unknown. The oldest grape seeds have been discovered at Orchomenos in the Middle Helladic deposit; other discoveries dating from the Late Bronze Age have been published.[10*] The importance of the seeds found at Orchomenos is increased by the fact that they were found in association with a pithos, together with grains of wheat; it seems almost certain that we have here the remains of wine. It is possible that the presence of the wheat grains is to be explained by supposing that the pithos had been used for storing grain or grain liquor before it was used for wine. Again, it is possible that a liquor was prepared from wheat and fruit juice, as is sometimes done today. Such scanty archaeological data, supplemented by philological data on the word *wine,* and a consideration of the place of wine in early Greek religion and of the geological and cultural relations of the Aegean peoples—these things together indicate that wine was known very early in the Age of Metals.

To summarize:

(1) Grapes and wine were known in Egypt during the Old Kingdom, that is, at a time corresponding to the Early Minoan Age. The close relations of the Cretans with Egypt make it likely that they would have imported wine and viticulture from there, even if they did not possess them already.

(2) Grapes certainly, and very probably wine were known in Greece in the Middle Helladic Period. It is likely that the new elements which entered Greece in this period were northern; hence grapes and wine were scarcely among them. Probably they date from the Early Helladic Period at the latest. Thus the Cretans would have wine-using peoples on both sides of them, and with both of them they had close relations—commercial, ethnic, or both. This, together with the fact that wine is easily imported, and that it is something of which it is easy to learn the use, makes it almost certain that the Cretans used wine, even if they did not make it.

---

[21]*Civ. Eg.,* p. 188.
[22]A splendid example in stone is illustrated in Seager, *Mochlos,* pl. 5.

(3) The words for *wine* in Latin, Greek, and Western Semitic are independent borrowings from a third source, almost certainly from the language or languages of Asia Minor and the Aegean. If only Greek and Western Semitic were involved, it might be explained that the words were introduced late from Asia Minor. But their independent presence in Latin proves that people outside Asia Minor, but of the same culture area, spread its use as far west as Italy. These peoples must have been either Minoans or Etruscans. Even if they were the latter, we must admit that wine was used by coastal peoples of Asia Minor who had been in close contact with the Minoans; this in itself lacks little of being proof that the article and word were part of Aegean culture in general.[11*]

(4) Wine was used in the chthonic worship of the Greeks, inherited from their predecessors in the Aegean.[23] The conservatism of cults makes this a very strong argument that the use of wine dates from early in the Bronze Age. A wholly new cult, *e.g.* the Dionysiac, might be introduced, but an innovation would scarcely be applied to an ancient and established one.

The fruits and nuts, other than olives and grapes, proved through archaeological evidence to have been known to the prehistoric peoples of the Aegean are almonds, figs, pears, plums, and pomegranates. The Neolithic peoples may also have eaten acorns.[12*] Whether these fruits and nuts were all known and used everywhere in the Aegean world from the earliest times is a question that cannot be answered. At least the almond seems to have been so known, and the fig was known as early as Neolithic times on the mainland. The word for *pomegranate* is among those words believed to be of pre-Greek origin. The apple, it seems, should also be added to the list.[13*]

It is likely that the date palm, if artificially introduced into Crete, was brought there in Middle Minoan times, but it is probable that its fruit was not eaten; the probability is that, if the Cretans ate dates, they imported them. The date tree grows in Crete today and reproduces, but the dates do not ripen sufficiently to be palatable. This failure of the date to ripen in Minoan times is indicated by a design on a M.M. II jar from Knossos.[24] In this picture the fruit is represented as standing, and hence as unripe. Evans regards this as evidence that, as in modern times, dates did not ripen adequately in Crete.[14*]

---

[23]Cf. *Odyssey X*, 519, and *XI*, 27.
[24]*P. of M.* 1, p. 254, fig. 190; 2, p. 493, fig. 298.

NOTES

1. Neolithic millstones have been found in Crete at Knossos (*P. of M.* 2, p. 13), Miamù (*A.J.A.* 1897, p. 279), and Magasà (*B.S.A.* 11, p. 268). The stones found at Miamù and Magasà are true millstones—not crushers; those found at the latter site are fitted together, the upper stone fitting into a hollow in the lower. It is most unlikely that such a stone was used for any other purpose than grinding grain. On the mainland, where grain of Neolithic date has actually been found, similar grinders were in use. Millstones of Neolithic date were found at Tsani; others, of Third Thessalian Period (Early Bronze Age) date, were found on the same site associated with barley (*P.T.*, p. 146).

2. The evidence for cereal grains follows:

WHEAT

Neolithic.—(mainland only): Sesklo (*D.S.*, p. 359; *P.T.*, p. 73); Dimini (*D.S.*, pp. 105 and 360; *P.T.*, p. 85); and Olynthus (*Olynthus*, pp. 16 and 82). Impressions of wheat or wheat chaff of pottery, *Olynthus*, pp. 29 and 82.

Early Bronze Age.—(mainland only): Rachmani (*P.T.*, p. 53); Tsani (*P.T.*, p. 149); and Vardaroftsa (*B.S.A.* 28, p. 199). Anatolia: Hissarlik (*Z. für E. Ver.* 1879, p. 270; Virchow, *Troas*, p. 68; *Ilios*, p. 320: "Triticum durum var. Trojanum" as identified by Wittmack.

Middle Bronze Age.—(mainland only): Orchomenos (*Orchomenos*, p. 60); Drachmani (*P.T.*, p. 204; *Eph.* 1908, p. 94; *R.E.G.* 1912, p. 285); Marmariani (*P.T.*, p. 54; *D.S.*, p. 360). The wheat from the latter site was identified by Wittmack as *Triticum dicocceum* (*D.S.*, p. 360).

Late Bronze Age.—Crete: Knossos (*B.S.A.* 7, p. 21); Mallia (*Mallia* 1, p. 38); Palaikastro (*B.S.A.* 8, p. 316). Mainland: Mycenae (Schliemann, *Mycenae*, p. 94; *Pr.* 1886, pp. 75-76; *B.S.A.* 25, p. 49). Fouqué states that no wheat was found at Thera (*Santorin*, p. 128; cf. *Bulletin de l'Ecole française d'Athènes*, 1870, p. 201).

BARLEY

Neolithic.—(mainland only): Dimini (*D.S.*, p. 360); perhaps Sesklo (*op. cit.*, p. 359).

Early Bronze Age.—(mainland only): Tsani (*P.T.*, p. 149).

Middle Bronze Age.—Orchomenos (*Orchomenos*, p. 60).

Late Bronze Age.—Crete: Knossos, the Caravanserai (*P. of M.* 2, p. 105); Palaikastro (*B.S.A.* 9, p. 280). Cyclades: Thera and Therasia (*Santorin*, pp. 120, 121, and 128; Hiller von Gaertringen, *Thera*, p. 40). Mainland: Mycenae (*B.S.A.* 25, p. 49).

MILLET (mainland only)

Neolithic.—Olynthus (*Olynthus*, p. 82).

Middle Helladic.—Marmariani (*D.S.*, p. 360; *P.T.*, p. 54). It was found matted together in such a way as to indicate that it had been made into a sort of bread.

MISCELLANEOUS

Early Bronze Age.—"Grain" (Hagia Marina: see *R.E.G.* 1912, p. 262).

Middle Bronze Age.—A single oat grain was found at Orchomenos (*Orchomenos*, p. 61). "Grain" was found in the Kamares Cave (*B.S.A.* 19, p. 11).

Late Bronze Age.—Dumont and Chaplain (*Céramique de la Grèce propre*, p. 31) mention rye among the grains found at Thera, but I have not been able to trace the source of this statement. Rye is said to have been unknown in ancient Greece (Jardé: *Les Céréales dans l'Antiquité grecque*, p. 4).

Grain, of which the kind is not specified, is said to have been found in the Temple Repositories at Knossos (*B.S.A.* 9, p. 41), and at Phaestos (*M.A.* 12, p. 43; *R.A.L.* 10(1901), p. 267).

3. Evidence on agricultural implements:

Crete.—Picture of a fork, perhaps a winnowing fork, on the Harvester Vase (*M.A.* 13, pp. 77 ff.; *P. of M.* 2, p. 47; Hall, *Bronze Age*, p. 156).

Cyclades.—Flint sickle teeth (*Phylakopi*, p. 224); Bronze sickle (*Bulletin de l'Ecole française d'Athènes*, 1870, p. 201; Perrot et Chipiez, *Histoire de l'Art* 6, p. 199; *Phylakopi*, p. 224).

Mainland.—Bronze sickle (*Zygouries*, p. 203, fig. 190, 2).

Anatolia.—Bronze blade, perhaps a sickle (*Ilios*, p. 604, no. 1418).

4. Wace and Thompson's objection to considering these structures ovens is that "it is not easy to imagine a domed oven inside a house so small as this. . ."; they add that modern domed ovens in Greece are always out of doors (*P.T.*, p. 37, note 1). Mylonas objects to accepting these structures as ovens because of the lack of a fire-box (*Olynthus*, p. 17). But compare the article in Daremberg-Saglio under the word *Furnus.*

5. Glotz (*Civ. Eg.*, p. 187) stated that dry vegetables formed a more important part of the diet than cereals.

6. Remains of vegetables:

BEANS

Early Bronze Age.—(mainland only): Hissarlik (Virchow, *Troas*, pp. 68-69).

Middle Bronze Age.—(mainland only): Orchomenos (*Vicia faba, Orchomenos*, p. 60).

Late Bronze Age.—Crete: Knossos (*B.C.H.* 4(1880), pp. 124 ff. and 127, note 2; *B.S.A.* 6, p. 21; Egyptian beans (so-called by workmen) *B.S.A.* 7, pp. 20-21, and *P. of M.* 2, p. 54); Nirou Chani, broad beans (*Eph.* 1922, p. 9 and *P.of M.* 2, p. 281).

LENTILS

Early Bronze Age.—(mainland only): Rachmani (*P.T.*, p. 53).

Late Bronze Age.—Mallia (*Mallia* 1, pp. 16 and 38); Thera (*Santorin*, p. 120).

PEAS

Early Bronze Age.—(mainland only): Rachmani (*P.T.*, p. 53); Gona (*B.C.H.* 41, p. 245. The peas were identified by M. Dauphiné of Paris); Hissarlik (*Ilios*, p. 320, note 11).

Middle Bronze Age.—(mainland only): Orchomenos (*Ervum ervilia, Orchomenos*, p. 60).

Late Bronze Age.—Crete: Knossos (*B.C.H.* 4(1880), pp. 124 ff.; *B.S.A.* 6, p. 21); Palaikastro (*Pisum sativum* L. and *Pisum elatius* M.B., *B.S.A.* 8, p. 316; cf. *B.S.A.* 9, p. 292, and the pod-bearing plant on a L.M. II vessel, *B.S.A.* 11, p. 285, fig. 15); Hagia Triada (*Memorie del reale Istituto lombardo*, vol. 21, p. 244, small peas and chick peas); Gournià (*Gournià*, p. 23). Cyclades: Thera (*Santorin*, pp. 120 and 128; H. von Gaertringen, *Thera*, p. 40).

VETCH

Early Bronze Age.—(mainland only): Vardaroftsa (*B.S.A.* 28, p. 199, wild vetch); Hissarlik (*Ilios*, p. 320 "bitter vetch"; Virchow, *Troas*, p. 68).

Middle Bronze Age.—(mainland only): Orchomenos (*Orchomenos,* p. 60); Sesklo (*D.S.,* p. 359).

Late Bronze Age.—*Crete:* Nirou Chani (*Eph.* 1922, p. 9; *P. of M.* 2, p. 281). *Mainland:* Mycenae (Schliemann, *Mycenae,* p. 99; *B.S.A.* 25, p. 49).

MISCELLANEOUS

Unidentified leguminous vegetables datable as Early Bronze Age were discovered at Hagia Marina (*R.E.G.* 1912, p. 262).

7. Names of vegetables probably of pre-Greek origin:

CELERY: σέλινον. (For the definition of σέλινον as celery see the article under *Eppich* in *P.W.* by Olck. He defends the definition at length.) Boisacq, following Sommer, suggests an etymology from the same root as ἑλίω, but he does not claim that it is correct. Leo Meyer states that its origin is uncertain. Cuny lists it as a pre-Greek word under his third category.

CHICORY: σέρις. Boisacq and L. Meyer state that its origin is uncertain; Curtius omits it. It is listed by Glotz as a pre-Greek word.

CUCUMBER: σίκυος or σίκυς. Compare the geographical name Σικυών. Boisacq suggests that it is a Thraco-Phrygian loan word; L. Meyer states that its origin is uncertain; Cuny suggests that it may be non-Greek, and classes it in his third category.

GARLIC: σκόρ[ο]δον. Boisacq gives no etymology, rejecting suggested connections with the Sanscrit which L. Meyer considers probable.

LEEK: πράσον. Boisacq, L. Meyer, and Curtius regarded the word as Indo-European. Cuny listed it as pre-Greek in his second category.

PEA: πίσος. Boisacq says that the word's origin is obscure and probably foreign; he suggests Thraco-Phrygian. L. Meyer also states that its origin is obscure. Cuny treats it as pre-Greek, belonging in his second category (*R.E.A.* 1910, p. 157).

CHICK PEA: ἐρέβινθος. Compare Erebinthodes, an unknown island in the Propontis named by Pliny (*N.H.* V, 151). It is regarded as a pre-Greek word by Boisacq, Kretschmer (*Einleitung,* p. 402), and Fick (*Vorgriechische Ortsnamen,* p. 153). Cuny regarded it as an Indo-European word to which the ending -νθ had been added. The existence of cognates in other Indo-European languages, which caused Cuny to take this view, is explained by Boisacq as due to independent borrowing. L. Meyer admits that it may be non-Greek.

PUMPKIN: κολοκύνθη or κολοκύντη. Boisacq says that the etymology is uncertain, and L. Meyer that it is not entirely understandable. The word is listed among pre-Greek words by Glotz.

RAMPION: σίσαρος. Cuny lists it as a pre-Greek word (*R.E.A.* 1910, p. 157); Glotz also classes it among pre-Greek words. L. Meyer states that the etymology is not understandable.

WATER PARSNIP: σίον. The word is called pre-Greek by Cuny (*R.E.A.* 1910, p. 157). L. Meyer states that its origin is not clear.

8. It would be superfluous to say anything in defense of the proposition that lamps were used in the prehistoric Aegean were it not for the fact that some authorities have denied that the vessels so identified are really lamps. E. Pfuhl (*J.A.I.* 1912, pp. 52-59), although he did not regard the later Greek lamps as derived from the Cretan and Mycenaean lamps, acknowledged that the latter were lamps, but A. Neuberger (*Technical Arts of the Ancients,* English ed., 1930, p. 236, third German ed., p. 240) denies that the Minoans or the Egyptians had lamps at

all. In support of the view that the objects in question are actual lamps, see Dawkins, *B.S.A. Supplementary Papers No. 1*, p. 138; Dussaud, *Civilisations préhelléniques*, second edition, pp. 116 ff.; Evans, *P. of M.* 3, p. 25; Xanthoudides, *Mesarà*, p. 14. The marks of fire around the wick slots of many of the examples is, in their case at least, conclusive evidence.

9. Evidence on the olive:

Early Cycladic.—Lamps and remains of oil (*Pr.* 1906, p. 88); lamps (*Eph.* 1899, p. 99 and fig. 27, pl. 9, no. 29).

Early Minoan.—Lamps (*Mesarà*, pp. 14, 52, 63, and 71).

Middle Minoan.—Olive press, date not certain (*B.S.A.* 8, pp. 306-308). Lamps: Chamaïzi (*Eph.* 1906, p. 149); Sphoungaras (*Sphoungaras*, p. 54, fig. 27f); Gournià, (*Gournià*, p. 3 and pl. 2, no. 68); Mesarà (*Mesarà*, pp. 53 and 63. Some of these lamps show signs of burning around the mouth). Hieroglyphic olive sign (*S.M.*, p. 219, no. 101; *P. of M.* 2, p. 269). Picture of olive spray and a ship on a signet, and a design of the olive tree on pottery (*P. of M.* 1, p. 262, fig. 194g).

Late Minoan.—Physical remains: Knossos, in L.M. III context, spring chamber (*P. of M.* 2, pp. 134-135); Lilianà near Phaestos (*R.A.L.* 11(1902), p. 331; *M.A.* 14, p. 635); Palaikastro (*B.S.A.* 9, pp. 280 and 288). Olive press: Palaikastro (*B.S.A.* 11, pp. 276-277 and fig. 8). Mrs. Hawes states that no olive press was found at Gournià, and suggests that the press was located outside the town (*Gournià*, p. 28). The so-called olive press in the palace at Knossos is not correctly so named (*P. of M.* 1, p. 378; 2, p. 543).

Settling vats for separating oil and water: Gournià (*Gournià*, p. 27, fig. 11; p. 28 and pl. 1, no. 14); Palaikastro (*B.S.A.* 9, p. 288). Note that both at Gournià and Palaikastro a pithos was found in connection with the settling vats in such a position as to catch the liquid as it ran out.

Lamps: Knossos, Zapher Papoura tomb no. 14 (*Archaeologia* 59(1905), p. 424, or *Prehistoric Tombs*, p. 39, fig. 35a, and p. 40); Phaestos (*M.A.* 12, p. 99 and figs. 33 and 34, no. 5); Hagia Triada (*R.A.L.* 11(1902), p. 437); Nirou Chani (*Eph.* 1922, p. 14, fig. 11); Sphoungaras (*Sphoungaras*, p. 54, fig. 27h); Gournià (*Gournià*, p. 30, pl. 2, nos. 55-58, 68-69, and 75-77; p. 36, pl. 5, nos. 26-29); Palaikastro (*B.S.A.* 8, p. 314; 9, p. 282; and 12, p. 5).

Representations in art: Frescoes: Knossos (*B.S.A.* 6, p. 47; 7, p. 26; *P. of M.* 1, p. 426; 3, p. 67 and pl. 18; *ibid.*, pp. 167 ff.); sarcophagus of Hagia Triada (*M.A.* 19, p. 42); painted pithos from Knossos (*P. of M.* 3, p. 422 and fig. 244); painted pithos from Pseira (*Pseira*, p. 26 and pl. 7; *P. of M.* 2, p. 476 and fig. 284; Hall, *Aegean Archaeology*, p. 98); alabastron from Palaikastro (*B.S.A. Supplementary Papers No. 1*, p. 37); the Vapheio cups (*Eph.* 1889, p. 159 and pl. 9; *op. cit.*, 1891, p. 15; *P. of M.* 3, p. 184); discussion of the olive motif (*P. of M.* 2, pp. 474 f.).

Miscellaneous evidence: Evans points to the absence of remains of grain and the like in the pithoi in the magazines at Knossos as evidence that they once contained liquids (*B.S.A.* 7, p. 45). The blackening of the walls of some of the *Kaselles* is evidence that they contained oil which burned fiercely when the palace was destroyed (*B.S.A.* 7, p. 48). A jar found at Mochlos was burned inside and out as though from the same cause (*A.J.A.* 1909, p. 300). Jars of the type associated with oil were found at stà Vissarà, Trypeti, and Komò—points on the route from Knossos to the south of Crete, and therefore evidence of the oil trade (*P. of M.* 2, pp. 71, 83, and 88 respectively).

Late Cycladic.—Physical remains: Thera (*Santorin*, pp. 97 and 121). Olive press: Thera (*Santorin*, p. 104; H. von Gaertringen, *Thera*, p. 40).

Late Helladic.—Physical remains: Mycenae (*Eph.* 1888, p. 136; 1891, p. 16, note 1; *B.S.A.* 25, p. 48); Tiryns (*Eph.* 1891, note 1).

Lamps: Grave near the Argive Heraeum (*M.A.I.* 1878, p. 285, no. 78); Vapheio tomb (*Eph.* 1889, p. 152); Kakovatos (*M.A.I.* 1909, p. 298).

Representations in art: fresco at Tiryns (Rodenwaldt, *Tiryns* 2, p. 20, no. 27, and pl. 3, no. 5); relief at Mycenae (*P. of M.* 3, pp. 194-195 and fig. 133). For the latter art, see Late Minoan, above.

10. Bulle, *Orchomenos,* p. 61: "Von besonderem Interesse ist, dass bei dem Pithos P² 70, neben einigen Weizenkornern 6 Traubenkerne gefunden wurden, diese also sicher aus ältermykenischen [*i.e.* Middle Helladic] Zeit."

The discoveries of Late Bronze Age date relating to the grape are as follows:

Crete.—Structure described as wine-press: Palaikastro (*B.S.A.* 9, p. 295).

Representations in art: seal from Thisbe (*J.H.* 1925, p. 11, no. 7); seal from Mycenae (*ibid.*).

Mainland.—Physical remains: Tiryns, large grape seeds identified by Wittmack (Schliemann, *Tiryns,* p. 83); Mycenae, settlings of wine in a jar (Hehn, *Kulturpflanzen und Haustiere,* 1911, p. 94 (editors' notes); Menelaion near Sparta, impression of grape leaves on a clay sealing of a jar (*B.S.A.* 16, pp. 9-10).

Representations in art: see *Crete,* above.

11. οἴνη, grape; οἶνος, wine: Boisacq regarded these words as pre-Greek, as did Meillet (*Histoire de la langue grecque,* p. 62). Curtius connected it with an Indo-European root. It was the opinion of Eduard Meyer that the word belongs to the Anatolian linguistic stock (*G. des A.* 1², 3rd ed., p. 705).

12. Archaeological discoveries of fruits and nuts (other than olives and grapes):

ACORN

Sesklo, in Neolithic context (*D.S.,* p. 359).

ALMOND

Neolithic.—Crete: from the Neolithic level below the palace at Knossos, an almond seed (*P. of M.* 2, p. 10). *Mainland:* (wild almonds) Sesklo (*D.S.,* p. 359); Dimini (*D.S.,* p. 360).

Late Bronze Age.—(Crete only), physical remains of almonds: Hagia Triada (*Memorie del reale Istituto lombardo* 21, p. 244).

FIGS

Neolithic.—(mainland only), physical remains of figs: Dimini (*D.S.,* p. 360); Olynthus (*Olynthus,* pp. 13 and 82).

Late Bronze Age.—

Crete.—Physical remains: Hagia Triada (*Memorie del reale Istituto lombardo,* 21, p. 244). Representations in art: fragment of pyxis showing a sacred fig tree and an altar, from Knossos (*J.H.* 1901, p. 102, fig. 2; *Klio* 5(1906), pp. 337 f.).

Mainland.—Physical remains: Kakovatos-Pylos (*M.A.I.* 1907, p. XIV). Representations in art: gold fig leaves, from Mycenae (Schliemann, *Mycenae,* pp. 191-192; *J.H.* 1901, p. 104).

PEAR

Early Helladic only.—Remains of wild pears were discovered in the Third Thessalian stratum at Dimini (*D.S.,* p. 360; *P.T.,* p. 85. The dating is not entirely certain.).

PLUM

A faïence model of a fruit, apparently a plum, was discovered in the Snake Goddess collection at Knossos (*B.S.A.* 9, p. 68, and fig. 45; *P. of M.* 1, pp. 499-500 and fig. 358).

POMEGRANATE

Some bone inlays representing pomegranate buds were discovered at Knossos, also in the Snake Goddess collection (*P. of M.* 1, p. 496 and fig. 354a).

13. μῆλον or μᾶλον: apple. Boisacq and L. Meyer say that its etymology is unknown; it is given as an Aegean word by Meillet (*Histoire de la langue grecque,* p. 304).

14. The date in Minoan art: the Vapheio cups (*Eph.* 1889, p. 161 and pl. 9; *Eph.* 1891, p. 15); gold ornament from Mycenae showing stags, apparently of the fallow deer, above date palms (Schliemann, *Mycenae,* p. 179, no. 265); the trees bearing the double axes on the Hagia Triada sarcophagus (*M.A.* 19, p. 29); a seal-stone from Palaikastro showing a palm, the Horns of Consecration, and a dog attacking a wild goat (*J.H.* 1901, p. 154, fig. 34; *P. of M.* 2, p. 492, note 2); a seal from Mycenae showing a palm tree and two long-horned bulls kneeling (*J.H.* 1901, p. 156, fig. 34; *P. of M.* 2, p. 494, note 2); seal from Mycenae showing what I believe to be a long-horned bull before a palm tree (*Eph.* 1888, p. 176, pl. 10, no. 14); a seal from Cephalonia showing a long-horned bull grazing in front of a palm (*Pr.* 1912, p. 256, fig. 17, and p. 267, fig. 50); a seal from Mycenae showing two wild goats and a palm tree (*Eph.* 1888, p. 178, pl. 10, no. 31); a larnax from Zapher Papoura (*Prehistoric Tombs,* p. 29); and a seal from Vapheio showing demons watering a potted palm (*Eph.* 1889, p. 169, pl. 10, no. 35 or *J.H.* 1901, p. 101). Evans (*J.H.* 1901, p. 101) gives this latter seal as evidence for the artificial introduction of the palm tree into Greece.

For a discussion of the palm-tree motif and a number of illustrations, see *P. of M.* 1, p. 254, and 2, pp. 493 ff.

VII

DOMESTIC ANIMALS

The peoples of the prehistoric Aegean, even in Neolithic times, kept sheep, goats, swine, and cattle.[1*] Except, perhaps, certain domestic fowls, they introduced no other animals during the Bronze Age to provide themselves with food.[2*] Bones of domestic animals have been found in such great quantities that one might be led to suppose that the people lived largely on meat. We have already noted the danger of making this error. Still, we know that they did eat the flesh of sheep, goats, swine, and cattle; at no time does there seem to have existed any religious tabu against any of them. Neither should we forget that animals, particularly the oxen, which drew the plow and perhaps threshed the wheat and barley played their part indirectly in feeding the people.

Goats and sheep furnished milk which, besides being drunk as sweet or soured milk, was used in the making of cheese.[3*] On certain seals of Middle Period date milk jars are shown suspended from poles—pictures, rare in Cretan art, giving details of an occupation.[4*] There is no direct evidence of the use of cow's milk; it seems probable that such milk was used, but the numerical superiority of goats, demonstrated below, must have made goat's milk much more common. Swine were important in the Bronze Age as a source of meat—more important, as will be shown, than they are today in the same region. They seldom figure in art, but a hog sign appears in the hieroglyphic signary.[1*]

The swine used throughout the Aegean world in the Neolithic Age and the Bronze Age are usually described as *Sus domesticus indicus*. The scientific identification for Cretan bones of Neolithic date is that of C. Keller; for those of the mainland, discovered in a cave on the island of Leukas, it is that of G. Velde.[1*] Remains of swine dating from various periods of the Bronze Age and discovered in various parts of the Aegean world have also come under scientific observation; there can be no doubt that the true domestic hog was known and raised in considerable numbers from Neolithic times onward. Something is known of the varieties of sheep and cattle then raised. The Cretans already possessed in Neolithic times peculiar varieties of sheep and cattle still common in the island.[1] Outside of Crete varieties of sheep do not seem to have been observed; the bones of cattle discovered on several northern sites and dating from as early as the Early Bronze Age have, however, been described as *Bos longifrons*.[1*]

---

*Numbers followed by the asterisk and enclosed in parentheses refer to notes at the end of the section; see page 69.
[1]*P. of M.* 2, p. 10; *Neue Denkschriften* 46(1911), p. 144.

One variety of ox is outstanding in Cretan and Mycenaean art—that frequently described by Sir Arthur Evans as the *urus*. Three types of cattle have been identified among the bones discovered on prehistoric Cretan sites: a small short-horned variety known as *Bos creticus*[2] and as *Bos brachycerus;* a large, long-horned variety, often referred to as *Bos primigenius* (the so-called *urus* mentioned above) ; and a medium-sized variety, probably a cross between the other two breeds. The latter, and, perhaps, the long-horned ox as well, would make a better beast of burden than the small short-horn which, however, seems to have been the most numerous variety in Crete. Was the long-horned ox a wild *Urochs*, or was it a domestic ox artificially introduced? If it was originally wild, was it ever domesticated? C. Keller called the animal *Bos primigenius*, but he believed that it was eventually domesticated.[3] E. Feige objects to the term entirely, and describes the animals in question as a breed of cattle very similar to the *urus*, but domesticated; he points out that there is no evidence for the existence of genuine wild cattle in the South.[5*]

The evidence for their domestication may be classified into three groups: (1) Representations of men capturing cattle alive; (2) Evidence of the long-horned oxen being kept in captivity; (3) Direct evidence of domestication. In the first category come the scenes showing bulls being thrown or taken in the open country; for example, Vapheio cup no. 1,[4] some sealings from Hagia Triada,[5] and the frescoes from the North Entrance of the West Gallery and elsewhere in the palace at Knossos.[6] In the second category come, first of all, the circumstances of the discovery of a quantity of bones and horns of these oxen in the palace at Knossos, the condition of which indicates that the animals were stabled there at the time when the building was destroyed,[7] and the fact that horns of oxen of this breed, including those of young animals, have been found with the ends cut off.[8] Further evidence is furnished by the existence of numerous representations in art of bull-leaping. Many of the scenes certainly picture not merely bull throwing, but true bull-leaping, a sport which could have been carried on only with captive or domesticated bulls. Among the best examples of such representations are the Toreador frescoes from Knossos.[9] Others are illustrated by Evans in connection with them, including a bronze figurine of a man being thrown over a bull.[10] Another type of picture connecting long-horned cattle with the

[2]Boyd Dawkins in the *Proceedings of the Manchester Literary and Philosophical Society* 46(1902), p. xlviii.
[3]*Neue Denkschriften* 46(1911), p. 155.
[4]*Eph.* 1889, pp. 159 ff. and pl. 9.
[5]*B.S.A.* 8-9(1929), pp. 103-104, nos. 60 and 61.
[6]*P. of M.* 3, pp. 167 ff.
[7]C. Keller, *Vierteljarhesschrift* 54(1909), p. 430, and *Neue Denkschriften* 46(1911), p. 150.
[8]*Eph.* 1912, p. 232.
[9]*P. of M.* 3, pp. 209 ff.
[10]Originally published in *J.H.* 41(1921), pp. 247 ff.

bull ring is that showing a lion attacking a bull. This was a common motif on seal-stones. The probability of its being a scene from the bull ring is established by three facts: (1) The bull usually has the marked traits of the long-horned breed, indicating Cretan scenes; (2) The pictures are life-like, yet there is no reason to believe that there were wild lions in Crete; (3) One seal[11] shows the lion in such a scene with rings on its legs.[12]

The discovery of clipped horns, and the existence of a mixed breed of cattle crossed with the long-horns, established a strong presumption in favor of actual domestication; a few pictures give direct evidence of it. The second of the Vapheio cups shows a grazing scene in which a man ties a rope to the leg of an unresisting bull, while nearby a bull and a cow are paying more attention to each other than to the man. Surely these are not wild cattle, whatever their breed. Again, a fresco fragment from the miniature frescoes of Knossos shows elephant tusks above and behind an ox head of the long-horned type.[13] On the basis of this Evans suggests the use of such oxen for transporting goods imported from Egypt across the island—a practice which would indicate that the Cretan saw no incongruity in representing a long-horned ox as a beast of burden. It should be added, moreover, that the representation on a seal of a bull led by a man, if a long-horned bull and not one of the mixed breed is really intended, proves their domestication.

That the so-called *Bos primigenius* was capable of domestication is proved by the fact that it was, at least eventually, domesticated. The only reason that Keller gave for accepting the human introduction of the *Bos brachycerus* while denying that of the larger oxen is that the size and violent nature of the latter animal would make its transportation in small vessels difficult.[14] This seems rather inconclusive; two small bulls would make more bulk than one big one. A fair tentative conclusion from the archaeological evidence must essentially agree with that of Feige: the long-horned Cretan cattle constituted a domestic breed, probably artificially introduced, and kept for purposes of cult, sport, and probably also for crossing with smaller cattle to produce draught oxen of medium size and weight.

While no single collection of animal remains permits one to judge the relative importance of the different animals as sources of meat, the combined evidence from all the prehistoric periods of Greece and Crete

---

[11]From Evans' Thisbe Collection, *J.H.* 45(1925), p. 8, no. 3, and pl. 1, fig. 8.
[12]Other examples of this motif are *Archaeologia* 59(1905) or *P.T.*, fig. 101, no. 2 (a seal from the Zapher Papoura cemetery); *Eph.* 1907, p. 175, pl. 7, no. 98 (a seal from near Knossos); *Eph.* 1912, p. 216, pl. 16f (a seal from Tylissos); *A.D.* 3, p. 169, fig. 124 (a seal from Thebes); *B.C.H.* 1904, p. 388 (a seal from Deiras, not illustrated); *Eph.* 1888, pl. 10, no. 18 (a seal from the tombs at Mycenae); *Eph.* 1889, pl. 10, nos. 18 and 21 (seals from Tomb of Vapheio).
[13]*P. of M.* 2, p. 742, fig. 475.
[14]*Vierteljahresschrift* 54(1909), p. 426.

is sufficient to justify confident conclusions on this subject. In pre-historic times, as today, the sheep was the most important animal; the hog was almost as important, and in some places may have been even more so; next comes the goat, followed by cattle. This is precisely the order of importance decided upon by C. Keller on the basis of the animal remains from Tylissos and, except in the case of swine, it is the same as the order of importance today. There are approximately half a million sheep in modern Crete, to about 250,000 goats and 60,000 cattle. Keller had no figures on the number of hogs in Crete, but he says that they are important.[6*] The heavier forestation in the Bronze Age would lead one to expect more hog raising, and the evidence seems to bear out this supposition, thereby confirming the theory, otherwise well attested, that Crete and Greece then had more woodland than they have now.

These conclusions have been reached by attempting first to decide whether the larger or smaller animals were the more important, and then to decide which of the smaller ones held the first place. An examination of the various reports of discoveries of animal bones from the Neolithic Period onward shows no example of a deposit of the remains of food with no cult connection in which the bones of cattle are not accompanied by those of the smaller animals; on the other hand, those of the smaller animals are frequently not accompanied by those of cattle. Moreover, the excavators have frequently commented on the proportions of the different animals represented in the finds, and only in a few cult deposits have they said that the bones of the larger animals are more numerous. I shall cite a few examples:

C. W. Blegen (on the Neolithic deposit at Nemea): "Animal bones were numerous, chiefly from the small animals such as sheep and swine; but one huge joint must have belonged to a creature as large as a good-sized ox."[15]

C. W. Blegen (on the Early Helladic remains of animals on that site): "Sheep or goats and swine were certainly represented, and there were not a few huge teeth of larger animals."[16]

G. Velde (on the bones from the Choirospelia in Leukas): ". . . . handelt es sich bei der Mehrzahl der Knochen um das Hausschwein;. . . ."[17]

Chr. Tsountas (of the bone tools from Thessalian sites): ". . . . κατασκευασμένα δ'εἶναι τὰ μὲν ἐκ τῶν ὀστῶν διαφόρων ζώων—ἰδία προβάτων καὶ αἰγῶν πιθανῶς. . . ."[18]

Chr. Tsountas (on animal remains discovered on the Cyclades): "διέκρινα δὲ μεταξὺ αὐτῶν [the bones] ὀδόντας προβάτων ἢ αἰγῶν καὶ δύο ἢ τρεῖς βοῶν."[19]

[15] A.J.A. 42(1927), p. 439.
[16] Zygouries, p. 194.
[17] Z. für E. 45(1913), p. 1159.
[18] D.S., p. 355.
[19] Eph. 1898, p. 168.

Tsountas and Manatt (on the animal remains at Mycenae): "It may be safely asserted, however, that the bones of swine exceed in quantity those of any other animal, and only those of goats and sheep together equal them."[20]

A. J. B. Wace (on a deposit of bones in the Pillar Basement at Mycenae): ". . . . and contained . . . . a quantity of split and broken animal bones, chiefly of sheep and swine."[21]

J. Hatzidakis (on the finds at Tylissos): "'Εκ σωροῦ ὀστῶν εὑρεθέντων ἐν ταῖς ἀνασκαφαῖς ἠριθμήσαμεν 32 σιαγόνας προβάτων καὶ αἰγῶν ἡμέρων καὶ ἀγρίων, 17 δὲ σιαγόνας συῶν ἐπίσης ἡμέρων καὶ ἀγρίων."[22]

On the basis of the above evidence only, it is reasonable to conclude that the smaller animals occupied a more important place in the food supply of the Aegean peoples than cattle, and that the first place among the former belongs to sheep or swine. The choice between these is harder to make. The statement of Hatzidakis about the remains from Tylissos, together with C. Keller's conclusions based on a careful examination of the same remains, is that sheep come first, with swine a close second. Tsountas' conclusions in regard to the remains from Mycenae put swine first, as do Velde's for the Neolithic cave in Leukas. Perhaps the best solution can be reached from another angle. Swine, it is reasonable to suppose, were raised in greater numbers in the more thickly wooded parts of the country. In some such districts swine raising may well have been more important than sheep raising. On the other hand, in the Bronze Age the country had already been occupied for thousands of years, and the tendencies toward deforestation had been at work throughout this time, so that the forest stand, although almost certainly much greater than that of today, probably approached modern conditions more nearly than is generally supposed. Crete, with its older civilization, was probably less well wooded than Greece. And in Crete the more thickly settled parts of the country, such as the plain of Mesarà, would be unfavorable for hog raising. Therefore I believe that on the whole the sheep was more important, although it may have been surpassed in importance by swine in some parts of the country.[7a]

It is difficult to learn much about how the prehistoric Aegean people housed and cared for their livestock. The probabilities are that their practices were not very different from those found in the same countries today. For example, modern Cretans do not use dogs in herding sheep. It seems likely that if the custom had ever been known it would have persisted.[8a] Again, the finding of structures high in the hills leads to the surmise that then as today flocks were taken into the hills during the summer, and that the structures correspond to the shelters now built in

---

[20] *Mycenaean Age*, p. 69. [21] *B.S.A.* 25, p. 181. [22] *Eph.* 1912, p. 232.

similar locations.[9*] Von Lichtenberg gives as an example of this sort of place the ruins at Kavousi. Although the settlement on the site was post-Minoan, enough earlier ware has been found there to make possible his suggestion that there existed earlier a Minoan *Metochie*.[23] What an Aegean stable was like is shown by the one discovered in Thera, with its straw bedding and crockery pans for feed. As seems to have been the case in the Caravanserai at Knossos, the grain used as animal feed was barley.[24]

The duck or goose and the pigeon appear in Cretan art and in the hieroglyphic system.[10*] The latter served as a subject for seal designs, goldsmith's work,[25] and figurines. There is no evidence from Crete of the use of pigeons as food, but C. Keller believed that they were so used.[26] That they were eaten in other parts of the Aegean world is shown by physical remains. Considerable quantities of pigeon bones, apparently the remains of food offerings to the dead, were found in tombs on the island of Cephalonia,[27] and some small bones found in tombs at Mycenae may likewise be pigeon bones.[28] The use of geese and perhaps of goose eggs as food is indicated by the discovery of the shells of such eggs in a tomb at Thebes.[11*] The goose also appears in art, *e.g.* on a well-executed seal-stone from eastern Crete,[29] a seal from Abdou Pediada showing an indistinct image of two geese,[30] and a seal from the Tomb of Vapheio.[31] Vollgraff[32] describes the birds on this latter seal as ducks, but Tsountas describes them as "goose-like birds," and it must be said that they closely resemble the bird on the seal from eastern Crete described above. Another waterfowl of this general type is named by Vollgraff.[33] Most important are the birds on the vessel from Deiras described by Vollgraff.[34] These are probably the *Chenalopex aegypticus*, said by C. Keller to have been the only ancient Egyptian domesticated goose, and probably introduced into Crete in Minoan times.[12*] Now the Egyptian goose, certainly domesticated from ancient times to the present day in Egypt, is an ornamental rather than a useful bird. It is described as having beautiful plumage; it is not much larger than a good-sized chicken (male, 8-10 lbs.; female, 6-8 lbs.); in shape it resembles a duck; and it lays only one setting of eggs a year.[35] It was regarded as a sacred bird by the Egyp-

[23]See *A.J.A.* 16(1909), pp. 127 ff.
[24]*P. of M.* 2, p. 105; Santorin, p. 121.
[25]Cf. Schliemann's *Mycenae*, pp. 180, 235, and 267, nos. 267, 268, 345, 423.
[26]*Neue Denkschriften* 46(1911), p. 159.
[27]*A.D.* 5, p. 97.
[28]*Eph.* 1888, p. 130.
[29]*Loc. cit.*, 1907, p. 66, pl. 7, no. 66.
[30]*Loc. cit.*, p. 175, pl. 8, no. 106.
[31]*Loc. cit.*, 1889, p. 166, pl. 10, no. 19.
[32]*B.C.H.* 1904, p. 380. Vollgraff's reference is to Perrot et Chipiez, *Histoire de l'Art* 6, fig. 428, 18.
[33]Shown in Perrot et Chipiez, *Histoire de l'Art* 6, fig. 490.
[34]*Ibid.*
[35]See Edward Brown, *Poultry Breeding and Production*, 2, pp. 757 ff.; and Laymon and Slocum, *Ducks and Geese*, p. 160.

tians, and there is evidence that it may have been so regarded in the
Aegean world. Evans reports the discovery of a large number of objects,
apparently, judging by their context, connected in some way with cult,
which had holes just slightly smaller than the average hen's egg.[36] He
believed them to be egg stands. Now the Egyptian goose is small, and
presumably its eggs are little if any larger than large hen's eggs. While
these geese scarcely lay eggs enough to permit their extensive use as
food, if we suppose that they were sacred, not only the cult connections
of the egg holders, but the discovery of egg shells in tombs is explained.
That the goose was once held sacred fits well with its connection with an
omen in the *Odyssey*[37] where, in Penelope's dream, geese represent the
suitors destroyed by the eagle, *i.e.* Odysseus, and the ornamental character of the Egyptian goose is in keeping both with Penelope's fondness for
them and the fact that, apparently, she did keep them for ornamental
purposes. Nevertheless, they may have been used for meat, for the flesh
of the Egyptian goose is said to be good, and it is known that the Cretans
did not refrain from eating cattle, despite their connection with cult. The
eggs may have been eaten, but their scarcity must have made them a
luxury. It must be observed that, according to Keller,[38] the gray goose
was not introduced until Hellenic times.

Although the evidence for the domestication of the duck is less convincing than that for the goose, the raising of domestic ducks is neither
disproved nor improbable. The country around Lake Copaïs, for example,
is suitable for them, but our evidence is entirely from art, unless Keramopoullos' Theban eggs are really duck eggs, and with one possible exception
it is entirely Cretan in tradition. Today, at least, the climate of Crete is
unfavorable for duck raising, and few are raised.[39] On the other hand,
wild ducks are known today in Crete, and there is no reason for considering any representation of a duck as that of a domestic duck unless
there is something about the scene in which the bird appears to prove
that it is domestic. Only one seal-stone which I have studied may fulfill
this requirement. It is a gem from Knossos, referred to as follows: "On
another Knossian gem he (a priest) holds a bird, apparently a duck—
having possibly a votive significance."[40] But in this case, in view of the
fact that the Egyptian goose resembles a duck and that it seems to have
been a sacred bird, it is possible that the picture represents a goose. The
finest piece of work representing ducks (the dagger blade from Mycenae)
has obviously Egyptian scenery.[41] An alabastron from Tomb III of the
Double Axe Group[42] has a design of flying ducks showing Egyptian influence. Among other representations of ducks are the following: a seal-

[36]*P. of M.* 2, pp. 307 f. and fig. 178.
[37]*Odyssey*, XIX, 536 ff.
[38]*Neue Denkschriften* 46(1911), p. 160.
[39]*Ibid.*
[40]*B.S.A.* 7, p. 20.

[41]*P. of M.* 2, p. 361; 3, p. 114, with colored
plate facing.
[42]*Archaeologia* 65(1914), p. 16, fig. 23 *a* and *b*.

ing from Knossos;[43] a seal from eastern Crete;[44] a vessel with markings, apparently swimming ducks, from Hagia Triada;[45] a staff head from Asine;[46] gold and cornelian pendants from Knossos and Palaikastro;[47] and gold pendants, probably from Aegina.[48] In respect to these latter ornaments, A. J. Evans commented in the accompanying article[49] that the duck as a decorative element is especially characteristic of metal work of the Late Bronze Age and the Early Iron Age of Central Europe, and of the type of European culture to which the broadest extension of the word Halstatt has been applied. Chronology, however, would seem to exclude the hypothesis of extra-Aegean elements in the development in the Aegean of the duck-shaped ornament.

A bird appearing on a Middle Minoan seal-stone has been identified as a cock,[50] and Glotz regarded the name Zeus Velchanos as evidence of the existence of chickens in Minoan Crete.[51] One of the Zakro sealings is described as picturing two cocks facing across an altar.[52] The image, however, is very indistinct. Among the gifts pictured on the wall of the tomb of Rekhmara in Egypt is a head which, in my opinion, might be taken for that of a cock.[53] Certain objects discovered at Knossos, apparently egg stands, have holes for six eggs just the right size to hold a hen's egg and keep it from slipping through. The above, so far as I know, is the only evidence for the existence of chickens in the prehistoric Aegean. None of the pictures is so markedly that of the bird in question that we must accept it as such and, as has been explained above, it is unnecessary, in view of the small size of the Egyptian goose, to suppose that the Minoans had chickens in order to explain the egg stands. The only writer on Aegean antiquities who, to my knowledge, maintained that chickens were known in the Aegean region in the Bronze Age is Glotz. Keramopoullos[54] gives a considerable amount of evidence to prove the contrary. Hehn[55] maintained that they were introduced late; on the other hand it must be noted that the editors of the 1911 edition[56] point out that the chicken was known in Babylonia in the reign of Gudea (c. 2500 B.C.), and that there is an Egyptian hieroglyphic sign which may represent a chicken.[57] Orth[58] speaks of the chicken as being introduced into the Western World by the Persians. It was also C. Keller's view that the bird was unknown in Minoan Crete.[59]

The occurrence of such words of pre-Greek characteristics as κήρινθος, bee bread, and σίμβλος, hive, leads one to suppose that bee culture pre-

[43]B.S.A. 9, p. 55, no. 36.
[44]Eph. 1907, p. 183, pl. 8, no. 153.
[45]M.A. 14, pp. 685 ff.
[46]Arberättelse, 1925, pp. 48 f.
[47]B.S.A. 8, p. 38, no. 11.
[48]J.H. 13, p. 204.
[49]1892-1893, pp. 204 ff.
[50]J.H. 14(1904), p. 342.
[51]Civ. Eg., p. 194.

[52]J.H. 1902, p. 88, pl. 10, no. 128.
[53]P. of M. 2, p. 535, fig. 339, lower right.
[54]A.D. 4, pp. 94 ff.
[55]Kulturpflanzen und Haustiere, pp. 326 ff.
[56]Ibid.
[57]Ibid., p. 339.
[58]P.W., s.v., Huhn, p. 2251, lines 22 ff.
[59]Neue Denkschriften 46(1911), p. 159.

ceded by a considerable interval the first record of it, and existed in the early period.[188] Bee culture was practiced in early Egypt, and it is possible that it is among the elements of Egyptian civilization that were introduced as a result of the close contact of Egypt and Libya with Crete during the age of the Old Kingdom and earlier. When the Cretan hieroglyphic system was developed, it possessed a bee sign similar to the Egyptian.[148] It would be difficult to exaggerate the importance of the use of honey in cookery before the introduction of sugar, for, by providing artificial sweetening, it made possible a wide variety of sweets and fancy dishes. Honey ranks in importance with olive oil and vinegar.

NOTES

1. Evidence of domestic animals:

SHEEP

Neolithic.—
Crete: Phaestos (*Neue Denkschriften* 46(1911), p. 144; *M.A.* 19, pp. 11, 146, 147, and 149); Miamù (*A.J.A.* 1897, p. 297); Magasà (*B.S.A.* 11, p. 368).
Mainland: Chaeroneia (*R.E.G.* 1912, p. 264); Nemea (*A.J.A.* 1927, p. 439); Olynthus (*Olynthus*, p. 5); and Leukas (*Z. für E.* 1913, p. 1159); Krasì Pediados (*A.D.* 1929, p. 124, note 2).

Early Bronze Age.—
Cyclades: Amorgos, sheep or goats (*Eph.* 1898, pp. 166-167); Paros, sheep or goats (*Eph.* 1898, p. 175); Syros (*Eph.* 1899, p. 105; sheep or goats, p. 126).
Mainland: Orchomenos, sheep or goats (*Orchomenos*, p. 29); Zygouries, sheep or goats (*Zygouries*, p. 194); Vardino (*Liverpool Annals* 12, p. 31); Hagios Mamas, sheep or goats (*B.S.A.* 29, p. 155); Molyvopyrgo (*B.S.A.* 29, p. 175); and Hissarlik (*Z. für E. Ver.* 1879, p. 269; Virchow, *Troas*, p. 62; *Ilios*, p. 322; *Troja*, p. 349); Saratsé (*B.S.A.* 30, p. 147, sheep or goats).

Middle Bronze Age.—
Crete: Tylissos, Cretan sheep (*Eph.* 1912, p. 231); Kato Mesarà (*A.D.* 9, p. 74, perhaps intrusive); Praesos (*A.J.A.* 16(1901), p. 378).
Cyclades: Phylakopi (*B.S.A.* 17, p. 6, two teeth of sheep or goat in a pithos-burial of a child).
Mainland: Mycenae (*B.S.A.* 25, p. 178); Vardino (*Liverpool Annals* 12, p. 31); Saratsé (*B.S.A.* 30, p. 147: sheep or goats).
In addition to the physical remains one should note, for the Middle Period, a seal from the Hieroglyphic Deposit at Knossos showing a horned sheep giving suck to a child (*P. of M.* 1, p. 273 and fig. 202e, figurines of sheep in the Kamares style discovered at Palaikastro (*B.S.A.* 9, p. 377), and the sheep sign in the hieroglyphic signary (*S.M.*, p. 207, no. 67).

Late Bronze Age.—
Crete: Palaikastro (*B.S.A.* 8, p. 314); Tylissos (*Eph.* 1912, p. 231; *Neue Denkschriften* 46(1911), p. 162).
Cyclades: Thera (*Bulletin de l'Ecole française d'Athènes* 1870, pp. 188 and 190; *Santorin*, pp. 103, 114, and 121).

Mainland: Mycenae (*Eph.* 1888, p. 130; *Mycenaean Age,* p. 69; *B.S.A.* 25, pp. 157 and 181); Thebes (*Eph.* 1909, p. 104); Messeniaki tou Pylou (*Eph.* 1914, p. 102); Dendrà (*Art and Archaeology* 25(1928), p. 283; *A.R.W.* 27(1929), p. 388); Chalcis (*Euboea,* pp. 26 and 39); Cephalonia (*Pr.* 1912, p. 117; *A.D.* 5, p. 97); and Vardino (*Liverpool Annals* 12, p. 31).

GOATS

Neolithic.—
Crete: Knossos (*P. of M.* 2, p. 10); Phaestos (*M.A.* 19, p. 163); Miamù (*A.J.A.* 1897, p. 297); Magasà (*B.S.A.* 11, p. 268). The head of a goat figurine was found at Knossos (*P. of M.* 1, p. 44 and fig. 11).
Mainland: Chaeroneia (*R.E.G.* 1912, p. 264); Hagia Marina (*R.E.G.* 1912, p. 278).

Early Bronze Age.—
Cyclades: see *sheep,* above.
Mainland: Orchomenos, Zygouries, and Hagios Mamas, see *sheep,* above; Vardaroftsa (*B.S.A.* 27, p. 45); Molyvopyrgo, identification uncertain (*B.S.A.* 29, p. 175); Hissarlik (*Z. für E. Ver.* 1879, p. 269; Virchow, *Troas,* p. 62; *Ilios,* p. 322; *Troja,* p. 349).

Middle Bronze Age.—
Crete: Tylissos (*Eph.* 1912, p. 231); Mallia (*Pr.* 1919, p. 58).
Cyclades: see *sheep,* above.
Mainland: Zygouries, the skeletons of two goats (*Zygouries,* p. 41); Molyvopyrgo (*B.S.A.* 29, p. 175).

Late Bronze Age.—
Crete: Palaikastro (*B.S.A.* 8, p. 314); Tylissos (*Eph.* 1912, p. 231; *Neue Denkschriften* 46(1911), p. 162); Psychro Cave (*J.H.* 17(1897), p. 355; *Proceedings of the Manchester Literary and Philosophical Society* 46(1902), p. xlviii; *P. of M.* 1, p. 627). Prints of goat hoofs in brick have been reported from Mochlos (*A.J.A.* 1909, p. 281), and Nirou Chani (*Eph.* 1922, p. 9).
Cyclades: Thera (*Bulletin de l'Ecole française d'Athènes* 1870, pp. 188 and 201; *Santorin,* pp. 103, 114, 120, and 121).
Mainland: Mycenae (*Mycenaean Age,* p. 69); Thebes (*Eph.* 1909, p. 104); Dendrà (*Art and Archaeology* 25 (1928), p. 283; *A.R.W.* 27(1929) p. 388); Chalcis (*Euboea,* pp. 26 and 39); Cephalonia (*Pr.* 1912, p. 117); and Vardaroftsa (*B.S.A.* 27, p. 45).

SWINE

Neolithic.—
Crete: Knossos (*P. of M.* 2, p. 10); Phaestos (*Neue Denkschriften* 46(1911), p. 144).
Mainland: Chaeroneia (*R.E.G.* 1912, p. 368); Hagia Marina (*R.E.G.* 1912, p. 278); Nemea (*A.J.A.* 1927, p. 439); and Leukas (*Z. für E.* 1913, p. 1159).

Early Bronze Age.—
(Mainland only): Zygouries (*Zygouries,* p. 194); Leukas (*Alt-Ithaka,* pp. 221, 232, and 240); Vardino (*Liverpool Annals* 12, p. 31); Hagios Mamas (*B.S.A.* 29, p. 150); Molyvopyrgo (*B.S.A.* 29, p. 175); and Hissarlik (*Z. für E. Ver.* 1879, p. 269; Virchow, *Troas,* p. 62; *Ilios,* p. 322); Krasì Pediados (*A.D* 1929, p. 124, note 2); Saratsé (*B.S.A.* 30, p. 147).

Middle Bronze Age.—
Crete: Tylissos (*Eph.* 1912, p. 231: *Sus domesticus indicus*).
Mainland: Mycenae (*B.S.A.* 25, p. 178); Vardino (*Liverpool Annals* 12, p. 31); Hagios Mamas (*B.S.A.* 29, p. 155); Saratsé (*B.S.A.* 30, p. 147).

Pictures of swine occur on a few seal-stones, and some figurines of swine have been discovered; they are, however, of little significance. More important is the fact that the hog appears in the hieroglyphic signary (*S.M.*, p. 208, no. 69; *P. of M.* 1, p. 282, fig. 214; *Gournià*, p. 55).

Late Bronze Age.—
Crete: Tylissos, *Sus domesticus indicus* (*Eph.* 1912, p. 231; *Neue Denkschriften* 46(1911), p. 161); near Knossos (*Vierteljahresschrift* 54(1909), p. 247); Psychro Cave (*P. of M.* 1, p. 627; *Proceedings of the Manchester Literary and Philosophical Society* 46(1902), p. xlviii).
Cyclades: Paros (*M.A.I.* 42(1917), p. 13 and fig. 79; Thera (H. von Gaertringen, *Thera*, p. 40; Dussaud, 2nd ed., p. 95).
Mainland: Mycenae (Schliemann, *Mycenae*, p. 99; *Mycenaean Age*, p. 69; *B.S.A.* 25, pp. 157 and 181); Thebes (*Eph.* 1909, p. 104; *A.D.* 5, p. 196); Chalcis (*Euboea*, pp. 26 and 39); and Vardino (*Liverpool Annals* 12, p. 31).

CATTLE

Neolithic.—
Crete: Knossos (*P. of M.* 2, p. 10), Cretan short horn and long horn (*Vierteljahresschrift* 54(1909), p. 430); Phaestos (*Neue Denkschriften* 46(1911), p. 144; *M.A.* 19, p. 141).
Mainland: Chaeroneia (*R.E.G.* 1912, p. 264); Hagia Marina (*R.E.G.* 1912, p. 278); near the Heraeum (*A.J.A.* 1925, p. 418); near Nemea (*A.J.A.* 1927, p. 439); Olynthus (*Olynthus*, p. 5); and Leukas (*Z. für E.* 1913, p. 1159).

Early Bronze Age.—
Cyclades: Amorgos (*Eph.* 1898, p. 166).
Mainland: Zygouries (*Zygouries*, pp. 12 and 116, fig. 105); Rachmani (*P.T.*, p. 53 and fig. 28); Vardaroftsa (*B.S.A.* 27, p. 45); Saratsé (*B.S.A.* 30, p. 147); Vardino (*Liverpool Annals* 12, p. 31); Hagios Mamas (*B.S.A.* 29, p. 155); Molyvopyrgo (*B.S.A.* 29, p. 175, probably *Bos longifrons*); Hissarlik (*Z. für E. Ver.* 1879, p. 269; Virchow, *Troas*, p. 62; *Ilios*, p. 322, and *Troja*, p. 349).

Middle Bronze Age.—
Crete: Tylissos, *Bos brachycerus, Bos domesticus,* and *Bos primigenius* (*Eph.* 1912, p. 231); Mallia (*Pr.* 1919, p. 58).
Mainland: Drachmani (*Eph.* 1908, p. 94; *P.T.*, p. 204); Vardaroftsa (*B.S.A.* 27, p. 45); Vardino (*Liverpool Annals* 12, p. 31); Hagios Mamas (*B.S.A.* 29, p. 155); and Molyvopyrgo (*B.S.A.* 29, p. 175).

Evidence on the breeding of cattle is furnished by the bowl containing figurines from Palaikastro (*B.S.A.* 8, p. 294; *P. of M.* 1, pp. 180-181 and fig. 130). An ox hoof from the Town Mosaic (*B.S.A.* 8, p. 21; *P. of M.* 1, p. 309, fig. 288b) is probably part of a herding scene. At least one breed of cattle other than the long-horn is represented in the numerous pieces of art work giving simple pictures of cattle. Two types are represented in the hieroglyphic system (*S.M.*, p. 206, nos. 61, 62, 63, and 64; *P. of M.* 1, p. 281). The large type of ox figurines from Palaikastro probably represent Cretan short-horn cattle. For "rhytons" representing men grappling long-horned bulls, see *Mesarà*, pp. 40, 42, 62, and pl. I, XXVIII; XXX, no. 4309 and 5049; VII; XXXVII, nos. 5052 and 5053; *P. of M.* 3, p. 205).

Late Bronze Age.—
   Crete: Bos primigenius: Knossos (*P. of M.* 2, p. 301 and fig. 175; *Viertel-jahresschrift* 54(1909), p. 430; *Neue Denkschriften* 46(1911), pp. 150 ff.); Tylissos (*Eph.* 1912, p. 231; *Neue Denkschriften* 46(1911), p. 162); Cave of Zeus, Mt. Ida (*M.A.I.* 10(1885), p. 62; and Palaikastro (*Vierteljahresschrift* 54(1909), p. 430). *Bos brachycerus:* Tylissos (*Eph.* 1912, p. 231; *Neue Denkschriften* 46(1911), p. 162); Psychro Cave (report of a paper by Boyd Dawkins in the *Proceedings of the Manchester Literary and Philosophical Society* 46(1902), p. xlviii; *Vierteljahres-schrift* 54(1909), p. 429). Mixed breed: Tylissos (*Eph.* 1912, p. 231). Breed not specified: Praesos (*A.J.A.* 16(1909), p. 378); Palaikastro (*B.S.A.* 11, p. 287).
   Mainland: (Breed not specified) Mycenae (*Eph.* 1888, p. 130; *Mycenaean Age,* p. 69); Dendrà (*Art and Archaeology* 25(1928), p. 130); Thebes (*Eph.* 1909, p. 104); Chalcis (*Euboea,* pp. 26 and 39); Vardino (*Liverpool Annals* 12, p. 31); and Vardaroftsa (*B.S.A.* 27, p. 45).

   2. Horses must have been introduced from without, probably late in the pre-historic era, but they were always rare and must seldom, if ever, have been eaten. See *Fimmen,* pp. 114-116.

   3. Clay strainers have been discovered in Neolithic deposits in Thessaly. Others have been discovered in Bronze Age deposits in Crete, the Cyclades, and on the mainland (*P.T.,* p. 113; *B.S.A.* 8, p. 309, fig. 22, nos. 13, 14; *B.S.A.* 27, p. 17; *Gournià,* p. 30, pl. II, no. 21; *Korakou,* p. 31, fig. 45; *Ilios,* pp. 273, 556, and 606, no. 1427; *Troja,* pp. 134 and 153; *Civ. Eg.,* p. 191). A substance that may be the actual remains of cheese has been found in Therasia (*Santorin,* p. 122).

   4. On the domestication of goats and the use of goat's milk see the following seals, etc.: *J.H.* 14(1894), p. 337, figs. 55, 56, 57, 60, 67, and 68; *J. H.* 17(1897), pl. 9 (facing p. 326) nos. 1-5, and text on p. 331, no. 8 and text on p. 332; and *Eph.* 1907, pl. VI and p. 154, no. 10; pl. VI and p. 157, no. 20; and pl. VI, p. 164, no. 41. These are prism seals with several, usually three, faces. On many of the seals re-ferred to there is shown a pole from which jars are suspended, often carried by a man. Frequently goats are associated with them. Thus in *J.H.* 14(1894), p. 337, no. 55, face *A* shows a man carrying a pole with four vessels on his shoulders; behind him is a goat, and in front of him is a pitcher; face *B* represents an animal that resembles a dog; and face *C* a man sitting on a stool holding a vessel of the type usually shown suspended from poles. It is interesting to note that fish are sometimes represented on seals of the type. Simple representations of domestic goats without significant context are to be found on seals and other forms of art. There is a goat sign in the hieroglyphic system (*S.M.,* p. 207, nos. 65 and 66; *P. of M.* 1, p. 196, fig. 114; 2, p. 269, note 1).

   5. See *Petermanns Mitteilungen* 198(1928), pp. 12 and 63. On p. 63 he speaks of " . . . Knochenfunde des Urs, oder besser gesagt einer sehr urähnlichen primigenen Rinderrasse . . . " See also note 2, above.

   6. Statistics for 1921 showed the following number of domestic food animals in Greece (*Petermanns Mitteilungen* 198(1928), p. 63): sheep, 5,789,113; goats, 3,717,340; cattle, 675,497; and swine, 404,485.

   7. It is worthy of mention, as showing the value of that sort of tradition, that Agathocles of Babylon, quoted in *Athenaeus* 9, 37a, stated that the Cretans held the pig sacred (because it had suckled the infant Zeus) and would not eat it. This

statement is the more remarkable in view of the fact that it might well be supposed to refer to Minoan times, and that it was made by a fairly early author.

8. The herding of sheep without dogs seems to be made possible by the absence of wolves. I know of no sure proof that there were or were not wolves in Minoan Crete. The ancient tradition was that there had once been wolves there, but that Heracles had exterminated them (*Diodorus* IV, 17, 3). This, however, may be merely a story to explain the absence of wolves. Keller does not name the wolf among the extinct fauna of Crete (*Vierteljahresschrift* 54(1909), pp. 424 ff.)

9. R. von Lichtenberg, *Ägäische Kultur*, pp. 51-52; Glotz, *Civ. Eg.*, p. 192.

10. See *Scripta Minoa*, p. 210, no. 82. A vase in the form of a dove was discovered at Knossos (*B.S.A.* 6, p. 7), and a figurine of a white dove was shaped in the bottom of a cup of Kamares style from Palaikastro (*B.S.A.* 8, p. 294; *P. of M.* I, p. 181, fig. 130).

11. See Keramopoullos' article in *A.D.* 4, pp. 94 ff. On the egg shells see the above article, p. 100, and *A.D.* 3, p. 196.

12. Keramopoullos (*A.D.* 4, pp. 94 ff.) speaks of the birds on this vessel as ducks, a fact probably explained by the resemblance of the Egyptian goose to a duck. Compare also a fresco fragment from Tiryns said to represent the *Chenalopex aegypticus* (*Tiryns* 2, p. 19).

13. κήρινθος: cf. Κήρινθος, a city in Euboea. Boisacq records some attempts to give an etymology of the word, but regards none of them as successful. L. Meyer and Curtius point out a connection of κηρός with Latin, Lithuanian, etc. Kretschmer (*Einleitung*, p. 70) considers it pre-Greek. Compare Conway's remarks so identifying it (*B.S.A.* 8, p. 155); Cuny (*R.E.A.* 12(1910), pp. 154-155), who considers the cognates in northern languages loan words, originally from the Aegean; and Glotz's list (*Civ. Eg.*, p. 441).

σιμβλός, hive: Boisacq states that the etymology is unknown. L. Meyer does not attempt to give an etymology, and Curtius omits the word. It fits Cuny's third category. Glotz lists it among pre-Greek words.

14. See *Scripta Minoa*, p. 202, no. 52; *P. of M.* I, pp. 28 and 281.

VIII

SEA FOOD

The modern Cretans are fond of octopods, and eat a great many of them. Neither do they fail to utilize squid, shellfish, and vertebrate fish. What was the practice of their predecessors on the islands and elsewhere in the Aegean in the New Stone Age and in the various periods of the Bronze Age? Formerly a ready partial answer was forthcoming: the Homeric Greeks rarely, if ever, ate fish. But more recent study of the remains of the homes and settlements of the early peoples of the region has compelled a revision of this answer.

Shellfish shells are lasting; there can be no doubt that, in Neolithic times as later, shellfish were eaten.[1*] They, however, can never have been very important as a source of food. But the octopus and sepia have, in modern times, been of the greatest importance, and must have been equally plentiful then.[2*] Unfortunately, from the very nature of the case, no remains of cephalopods used as food have been discovered, and we have no evidence about them except in the hieroglyphic system and in art, and through the discovery of instruments that may have been used in catching them.[3*] But this evidence is sufficient to justify one in believing it probable that the Cretans, at least, made use of cephalopods from very early times—very probably in the Middle Minoan Period and almost certainly in the Late Minoan Age.

The people of the Early Cycladic culture fished for vertebrate fish. Barbless fish-hooks of bronze belonging to the Early Period have been discovered in Syros.[1] A barbless hook was also found at Phylakopi, but the report does not date it; apparently the circumstances of its discovery did not permit doing so. Certain weights belonging to the Macedonian Bronze Age discovered at Sedes may be net weights. The familiarity of the Early Cycladic peoples with the sea, fish, and navigation is proved by representations of ships with a fish ornament at the prow on certain vessels from Syros.[2] That the use of fish was not limited to the Cyclades in the Early Bronze Age is indicated by a gold bead in the form of a fish vertebra discovered at Mochlos[3] and, perhaps, by a bone of a *Lamna cornubica* Cuv., discovered in a tholos tomb at Krasì Pediados, which seems, however, to have been worn as an amulet.[4] Actual remains of fish were discovered at Hissarlik in considerable quantities. Among them were recognized vertebrae of large tunny fish and of a fish of the shark

---

*Numbers followed by the asterisk and enclosed in parentheses refer to notes at the end of the section; see page 76.
[1]*Eph.* 1899, p. 104 and pl. 10, nos. 30 and 39.   [3]Seager, *Mochlos*, p. 22.
[2]*Loc. cit.*, p. 90, and p. 92, fig. 22.   [4]*A.D.* 1929, p. 124, note 2.

family, and the teeth of a ray. Some of the remains of fish belonged to the oldest settlement on the site.[4*]

Even in the Troad, much less elsewhere, the relative importance of fishing to other means of obtaining food cannot be determined through the archaeological evidence. It is reasonable, however, to suppose that it was similar, even in the Early Bronze Age, to what it has been in later times. Not only has the invertebrate sea life of the Mediterranean not changed in recent geologic times,[5] but there is no reason to believe that the vertebrate forms of sea life have changed to any extent. It is just possible that religious motives may have increased the consumption of fish since the spread of Christianity, and this possibility would invalidate conclusions based on excessive dependence on modern analogies. But, given the fact that the Aegean peoples had the means of fishing, it is not too much to suppose on the analogy of later pre-Christian conditions, that fishing among them was already an industry rather than a sport or desultory occupation, and that fish entered into the diet of the people to a considerable, though not predominant, extent.

Fish appear in art during the Middle Minoan Period. Representations of flying fish have been found in Knossos, on seals in the East-West Corridor Deposit[6] and at Phylakopi in Melos.[7] Evans identifies certain signs in the hieroglyphic system as tunny fish.[8] If Glotz is right in his statement that tunny fishing involves large-scale operations,[9] the existence of this sign is of great importance; it proves that the Minoan peoples already were familiar enough with the tunny fish to draw it. This, taken with the fact that they fished for the tunny in the Late Minoan Period, practically constitutes proof that they already did so in Middle Minoan times. Fish designs of a less-marked type are not infrequent on seals of the age, frequently associated with milk goats.[5*]

For the Late Bronze Age the evidence is even more conclusive.[6*] There is some evidence for the Cyclades, and sufficient evidence for Boeotia on the mainland. It is probably not too much to say that the population of all the Aegean lands used vertebrate fish extensively, especially along the coast, and that now, at least, fishing was a trade, engaged in as a regular means of livelihood. The net weights from Thera are a further indication that this is true.

Such a conclusion is, of course, apparently contrary to the traditional view based on Homer, which Tsountas[10] believed was confirmed both by Schliemann's excavations at Mycenae and by his own,[7*] and which was accepted by Beloch.[11] Although, considering the evidence from Thebes,

[5]Philippson, *Mittelmeergebiet*, p. 60. [8]*S.M.*, pp. 204-205, no. 59.
[6]*B.S.A.* 7, p. 101. [9]*Civ. Eg.*, p. 197.
[7]The Flying Fish Frieze, *Phylakopi*, p. 70. [10]*Eph.* 1891, pp. 30 ff.; *Mycenaean Age*, p. 69.
[11]*Griechische Geschichte* 1¹, p. 302 and note 3, with reference to *Odyssey* IV, 368, and XII, 330, and to Tsountas' views.

it is no longer possible to doubt that fish were used, it does not seem very difficult to reconcile the established facts with Homeric tradition. We must simply remember that the nobles whose doings interested the poet were not the only Greeks; they were rulers over an ancient population whose ancestors had lived by the sea for ages. It could well be that for the nobles, in Beloch's words, "hatte diese Nahrung ungefähr denselben Widerwillen eingeflösst wie uns Nördländern die *frutti di mare.* . . .," despite their desire to imitate the Cretans. Still, this fact would not make it in the least less likely that the earlier inhabitants had the same habits in the matter as the Cretans and the peoples of the Cyclades. And it will be remembered that, even in the passages in the *Odyssey* cited to prove that dislike of Homeric Greeks for fish, the Homeric sailors appear familiar with the means of fishing and could use them in case of need. One should also mention another explanation of the reluctance of the heroes to eat fish. It is said that near Smyrna the fish are not fit to eat, and the poet, coming from that vicinity, was prejudiced against all fish.[12] In any case, the evidence from Homer need cause one no hesitation in accepting the implications of the discovery of the remains of fish and fishing tackle at Thebes.

NOTES

1. The invertebrate sea life of the Mediterranean has not changed since Neolithic times (Philippson, *Das Mittelmeergebiet*, p. 60), and the deposits show that people from then to our day have eaten about the same varieties. The following is a partial list of the discoveries of shells:

Neolithic.—
Crete: Miamù (*A.J.A.* 1897, p. 279) ; Magasà (*B.S.A.* 11, p. 266) ; Phaestos (*M.A.* 19, p. 147; *R.A.L.* 16, pp. 267 and 272) ; Knossos (*P. of M.* 2, p. 10). Among the shells discovered are *Unio pictorum,* sea crab, lobster (*Homarus vulgaris*), *Murex trunculus,* limpet, oyster, cockle, and whelk.
Mainland: Leukas (*Z. für E.* 1913, p. 1159) ; Olynthus (*Olynthus,* p. 5). No shells were identified, but it is said in the report of the discoveries in Leukas that the circumstances indicate the use of shellfish as food.

Early Bronze Age.—
Cyclades: Amorgos, limpet shells (*Eph.* 1898, p. 166) ; Paros, oyster, murex, heartshell, snail, limpet, and others (*Eph.* 1899, p. 73). The shells were not numerous enough, in the opinion of the investigator, to indicate that the people depended much on shellfish. That they used them to some extent, however, he had no doubt.
Mainland: Zygouries, snail and oyster (*Zygouries,* pp. 15, 16, and 21) ; the Troad (*Z. für E. Ver.* 1879, pp. 267-268; *Ilios,* pp. 114, 213, 269, and 322).

---

[12]John A. Scott in *Classical Journal* 12, pp. 328 ff.

Middle Bronze Age.—
Crete: Tylissos (*Eph.* 1912, p. 232) ; Phaestos (*R.A.L.* 11(1902), p. 531).
Cyclades: Phylakopi (*B.S.A.* 17, p. 6).
Mainland: Mycenae (*B.S.A.* 25, p. 178).

Late Bronze Age.—
Crete: Tylissos (*Eph.* 1912, pp. 232-233).

2. Tsountas wrote (*Eph.* 1898, p. 200, note 4) that at that time the yearly catch of octopods in Antiparos was 25,000 kilograms, about half of which were caught by fishermen using eight boats, and the rest from the shore.

3. Evidence for the use of cephalopods as food:

NAUTILUS

Edibility: see *Grand Larousse universel,* p. 872, col. 1 (s.v.) " . . . sa chair est dure, coriace: cependant, sur les côtes de la mer des Indes les habitants la boucanent et en font provision."

Evidence that it was eaten in ancient Greece: see *Athenaeus* VII, 317b (quoting Clearchus): "Περὶ δὲ Τροιζῆνα τὸ παλαιὸν φησιν ὁ αὐτὸς Κλέαρχος οὔτε τὸν ἱερὸν καλούμενον τουλύπουν νόμιμον ἦν θηρεύειν, ἀλλ'ἀπεῖπον τούτων τε καὶ τῆς θαλαττίας χελώνης μὴ ἄπτεσθαι." Cf. Tsountas' comment on this passage (*Eph.* 1898, p. 202, note 2).

Representations in art: see Reisinger, *Kretische Vasenmalerei,* p. 27, where he identifies the nautilus represented as the *Argonauta argo.* Examples: vase in Marseilles (*J.A.I.* 1893; *Anzeiger,* p. 9; *P. of M.* 2, p. 509, fig. 312a) ; jar in the Museum of the Historical Society of New York (*A.J.A.* 6(1890), pp. 437 ff.) ; vase from Pseira (*Pseira,* p. 32, fig. 13).

OCTOPUS

Means of fishing: the usual method of fishing the octopus is with the multipointed fish spear ; see note 7.

Catching of the octopus: M.M. III seal from Knossos showing a man holding an octopus in one hand and a fish in the other (*B.S.A.* 7, p. 10; *P. of M.* 1, p. 677, fig. 497).

Miscellaneous representations of octopods: The octopus (or sepia) occurs on some Middle Minoan seals (*e.g. P. of M.* 1, p. 273, fig. 202), and is one of the most common designs in Late Minoan art. For illustrations of typical octopus vases see *P. of M.* 2, pp. 503 and 509. A fine octopus relief on a carved stone vessel was found in a tomb at Mycenae (*Eph.* 1888, pl. 7, p. 158). The following will illustrate the development of the design and give an idea of the interest in it and its distribution:

Middle Minoan III: Pachyammos (*Pachyammos,* pl. 13).
Late Minoan I: Palaikastro (*B.S.A., Supplementary Papers No. 1,* pl. 18).
Late Minoan II: Tomb of Isopata, near Knossos (*Prehistoric Tombs,* pl. 100) ; Knossos (*P. of M.* 2, p. 538, fig. 342).
Late Minoan III: Gournià (*Gournià,* pl. 10, nos. 12 and 45) ; and Milatos (*A.D.* 6, p. 158, figs. 5, 6, and 7). See also the floor design from Tiryns (*Tiryns 2, Taf.* 21) ; and certain gold ornaments from Mycenae (Schliemann, *Mycenae,* p. 181, nos. 270 and 271 ; p. 268, no. 424).

SQUID

The appearance of the squid in the hieroglyphic system has already been noted. Evans says of it: "The *Kalamari* is still the greatest marine delicacy in Crete, Greece, and Southern Italy." (*S.M.,* p. 205). It appeared frequently on Late Minoan seals, and had become a conventional design by M.M. III-L.M. I (*Sphoungaras*, p. 69). Examples are: a seal from Sphoungaras (*Sphoungaras*, p. 70, fig. 45c) ; *Eph.* 1907, p. 169, pl. 7, no. 51 (called by Xanthoudides a sepia) ; *op. cit.*, p. 172, pl. 7, no. 81 (called a sepia) ; p. 176, pl. 8, no. 105 (called a squid) ; p. 183, pl. 8, no. 157 (called a squid).

4. See *Z. für E. Ver.* 1879, p. 269; Virchow, *Troas*, p. 322; *Troja*, p. 349.

5. See note 4, page 72. The following are miscellaneous examples of seals and pottery (Middle Minoan) showing pictures of fish: *P. of M.* 1, p. 202b (a seal showing a fish and an octopus, either stranded or in a sea grotto; cf. Bruck, *Der Naturforscher* 2, p. 509, who asserts that the kind of fish represented cannot be determined) ; *B.S.A.* 19, pp. 15 and 19 (a fish design on a vessel from the Kamares cave) ; *Eph.* 1907, p. 154, pl. 1, no. 9 (a seal-stone) ; *J.H.* 17(1897), pl. 9 (facing p. 326), no. 8, face *C; P. of M.* 1, p. 182, fig. 131 (M.M. I polychrome pottery with fish designs) ; and *Sphoungaras*, p. 70, fig. 40c, a clay seal from Sphoungaras, described as older than Late Minoan, showing a whorl (*i.e.* a ring) of fishes. There is special interest in an ivory seal from Platanos (*Vaulted Tombs of Mesarà*, p. 114, and pl. 14, no. 1079) showing a ship, two fish beneath it, and a four-pronged object that may be a fishing spear. The seal belongs to the early part of the Middle Period, perhaps to E.M. III or M.M. I.

6. Late Bronze Age evidence of fish and fishing:

FISHING TACKLE

Crete: Gournià (*Gournià*, p. 34, pl. 4, no. 43: a lead sinker with a notch at each end, and an eye; *ibid.* no. 44: a piece of a large barbed fish-hook; *ibid.* no. 45: a barbed fish-hook, 7.2 cm. in length; *ibid.* no. 46: a barbed fish-hook, 2.6 cm. in length; *ibid.* no. 47: a barbed fish-hook, 9.5 cm. in length) ; Hagios Onouphrios (*M.A.* 13, p. 98, fig. 7: a two-pointed spear, perhaps for fishing).

Cyclades: Thera (*Santorin*, p. 124 and *Bulletin de l'Ecole française d'Athènes* 1870, p. 190: stone weights, apparently for nets).

Mainland: Thebes (*A.D.* 3, pp. 177-178, fig. 129: a bronze wire fish-hook, 4.5 cm. in length) ; Dendrà (*Art and Archaeology* 25(1928), p. 279 and fig. 280, a fishing spear) ; compare the object from the Fourth Shaft Grave (Schliemann's numbering) at Mycenae, which he described as a fork for stirring funeral fires (Schliemann, *Mycenae*, p. 255, no. 372).

PHYSICAL REMAINS OF FISH

Crete: Knossos (*B.S.A.* 7, p. 10 and *P. of M.* 1, p. 555: fish bones in a cooking pot) ; Phaestos (*M.A.* 12, p. 55) ; Tylissos (*Eph.* 1912, p. 233). Marinatos gives a list of undated remains of fish discovered in Crete in *A.D.* 1929, p. 133, note 2.

Mainland: Thebes (*A.D.* 3, p. 180, and 4, p. 91: fish vertebra identified as belonging to the class of fishes of which the *Perca fluvialis* is the type).

REPRESENTATIONS IN ART

EEL.—Knossos (*B.S.A.* 6, pp. 39-40: picture of an eel painted on the wall of a pool near the Throne Room; comment on the present renown of the eels of the Kairatos). On modern fishing of the eel, see Tsountas, *Eph.* 1898, p. 201.

FLYING FISH.—

Crete: Knossos (*P. of M.* 1, p. 521 and fig. 379: faïence models from the Snake Goddess Shrine) ; a seal from the Maurospelio cemetery (*B.S.A.* 28, p. 268) ; a seal (*P. of M.* 1, p. 677-678, fig. 499).

Cyclades: the flying fish fresco of Phylakopi (*Phylakopi*, p. 70; *P. of M.* 1, p. 541, fig. 393; *Naturforscher* 2, p. 509, fig. 8).

Mainland: Tomb of Vapheio, a gold inlay from a dagger blade (*Eph.* 1889, p. 151; *Essays in Aegean Archaeology*, pp. 63 ff.; *P. of M.* 3, p. 127, note 2).

MULLET.—named among the fish known to the prehistoric Cretans by Glotz (*Civ. Eg.*, p. 197).

SCARUS.—a small gold model from Knossos (*B.S.A.* 8, p. 81; *P. of M.* 3, p. 411); a seal from Knossos showing a man holding in one hand a scarus fish on a cord, and in the other an octopus (*B.S.A.* 7, p. 10; *P. of M.* 1, p. 677, fig. 497); and a seal showing a fish in a marine scene, identified as a scarus by Evans, but as probably a tunny by Bruck (*P. of M.* 1, p. 677, fig. 498; 3, p. 411, fig. 275; *Naturforscher* 2, p. 508).

TUNNY.—See Bruck's comment referred to under *Scarus*, above. Compare a seal from Cyprus (*J.H.* 17(1897), p. 65, pl. 3, no. 1); a seal from Melos (*ibid.*, no. 4); and a seal showing a man holding a tunny fish on a cord (*British Museum Catalogue of Gems*, 1926 edition, no. 40).

In addition to the seals showing fish held by people in such a way as to indicate that they had been caught, note the Fisherman's Vase from Phylakopi (*Phylakopi*, p. 123). Pictures representing unidentified fish and fish in no significant surroundings are not uncommon in Minoan and Mycenaean art.

7. Compare Keramopoullos' article on the eating of fish (*A.D.* 4, p. 88), and his remarks in the preceding volume of the same series (p. 179).

IX

HUNTING

To us, hunting suggests sport, not labor. Men go miles from home to shoot a deer whose flesh is not worth a fraction of its cost either in money or time. They hunt, not to get the deer, but to have the experience of getting it. The prehistoric people of the Aegean—if we except those who dwelt far from civilization—seem to have hunted from similar motives. Even the Neolithic inhabitants, to judge by the proportion of bones of wild animals to those of domesticated ones found in their settlements, depended on hunting very little. Never, however, did their successors in the Bronze Age give up the chase; instead, they developed it into a refined social event. The prominence of hunting scenes in Minoan art gives one a hint of how the subject must have interested the nobles.

Since it may not be supposed that any wild game was artificially introduced, it is certain that any animals hunted in later times were available to the Neolithic inhabitants; these are, chiefly, the wild boar, the deer, the wild goat, the rabbit, the hare, and waterfowl. Antelope and deer remains have been discovered on the mainland; remains of the wild goat have been discovered only in Crete, but the animal exists rarely on the mainland in modern times. The deer, now extinct in Crete, existed there throughout the Bronze Age. That the boar and the deer were hunted on the mainland, and that the rabbit (or hare) and the deer were hunted in Crete in Neolithic times is proved by discovered remains. The first hunting of hare and waterfowl on the mainland is proved for the Early Bronze Age; remains of the wild goat, then and later, at least, the most common object of the chase in Crete, first appear there in Middle Minoan context, and remains of swine certainly wild are known to occur there only in Late Minoan strata. The only remains certainly of wild game discovered in the Cyclades are those of the hare, discovered under the tufa in Thera.[1*] It seems likely, however, that the failure of some of these animals to appear in the earlier strata is due only to paucity of evidence, and that they were all hunted in the earliest times.

Our knowledge of the weapons and modes of hunting, except in their simpler forms, is based upon pictorial evidence; hence it goes back only to the Middle Minoan Period, and is best for the Late Minoan Age. The Neolithic peoples and those of the early Bronze Age had bows and arrows of some sort, and spears; that hunting dogs were used on the mainland in Neolithic times is suggested by the presence there of the remains of

---

*Numbers followed by the asterisk and enclosed in parentheses refer to notes at the end of the section; see page 81.

dogs. In Crete the presence of dogs is proved first for the Early Minoan Period by the figure of a Cretan hound on a steatite lid from Mochlos. The more complete evidence for the Late Bronze Age proves that then, at least, the hunt was highly organized. The conjecture that hunting was the sport of nobles and lords in Aegean antiquity is confirmed.

As has been remarked in connection with the boar-hunt fresco in Tiryns, ladies and gentlemen went to the hunt. The ladies went not merely as spectators; we see them on foot leading dogs as well. Nets were stretched. If the scene in Tiryns really represents a hunt on the mainland, we may believe that then, as later in historic times, Cretan hounds were imported for boar hunting. The hunters were armed with spears and bows, the latter sometimes of the highly efficient recoiling type. This equipment is elaborate and perfected; Keller's description of the weapons of the time as *primitive* should not be interpreted to mean *crude*. [2*] The chariot was used not merely for riding to the hunt; some pictures show hunters shooting game from the chariot. Another interesting practice is the use of the lariat as a means of capturing game alive—an instrument that seems also to have been used by shepherds in catching sheep. [3*]

The game was, of course, the same as had been hunted since Neolithic times; forms of game that have since become extinct were still to be found. That in Crete the chief animal was the wild goat is indicated both by the quantities of its bones found at Tylissos and by its prominence in art. It was probably also hunted on the mainland, for it seems to have existed there, but no prehistoric remains have been reported. Next in importance, in Crete, came the wild boar; on the mainland it was probably the most important game animal. Another very important animal was the deer, which still existed in Crete. Hunting was certainly a major interest among the upper classes, and it probably provided them with a considerable amount of food. Still, even they depended on domestic animals more than they did on the chase for their meat supply; the peasant and townsman must have depended on domestic animals almost entirely.

NOTES

1. Evidence on wild game:

ANTELOPE

Hissarlik, physical remains (Virchow, *Troas*, p. 64).

WILD BOAR

Neolithic, physical remains: Hagia Marina (*R.E.G.* 1912, p. 278); Chaeroneia (*R.E.G.* 1912, p. 264); Pyrgos (*P.T.*, p. 85); and Olynthus (*Olynthus*, p. 94).
Early Bronze Age, physical remains: Zygouries (*Zygouries*, pp. 27 and 192);

Leukas (*Alt-Ithaka*, p. 225); Vardaroftsa (*B.S.A.* 27, p. 45); and Hissarlik (*Z. für E. Ver.* 1879, p. 270; *Ilios*, p. 431, nos. 588-590).

Middle Bronze Age, physical remains: Aspis (dating not certain, *B.C.H.* 30(1906), p. 39).

Late Bronze Age.—Crete, physical remains: Tylissos (*Eph.* 1912, p. 231; *Neue Denkschriften* 46(1911), p. 161: *Sus scrofa ferus*); Zapher Papoura, perforated tusks, not certainly wild (*Vierteljahresschrift* 54(1909), p. 427). *Mainland*, physical remains: Mycenae (*B.S.A.* 25, pp. 56 and 303; *Mycenaean Age*, p. 69); tomb near the Argive Heraeum (*M.A.I.* 3(1878), pp. 277 and 285); Asine (*Ârberättelse* 1924-1925, p. 48); Dendrà (*Art and Archaeology* 25(1928), p. 282; Zygouries (*Zygouries*, p. 207); Kakovatos-Pylos (*M.A.I.* 34(1909), p. 292); Thebes (*Eph.* 1909, p. 104; *A.D.* 3, p. 80); Spata (*B.C.H.* 2(1878), p. 203); Vardaroftsa (*B.S.A.* 27, p. 45).

Representations in art: seal from eastern or central Crete (*Eph.* 1907, p. 176, pl. 8, no. 109); seal from Knossos (*Eph.* p. 164, pl. 6, no. 40a); fragment of carved steatite rhyton from Palaikastro (*B.S.A. Supplementary Papers No. 1*, p. 136; *P. of M.* 1, p. 675, fig. 496); hunting fresco at Tiryns (*Tiryns* 2, p. 123, fig. 55 and pl. 13; see also pp. 126 and 131); seal-stone from the Tomb of Vapheio (*Eph.* 1889, p. 165, pl. 10, no. 15); seal from the Peloponnese (*A.G.* pl. 2, no. 12); a seal representing a sacrifice scene, in which a boar has been placed on a table on its back and is being cut open with a knife by a person standing over it (*Eph.* 1888, p. 179, pl. 10, no. 36); a seal from the Peloponnese showing two boars lying side by side, perhaps in a swamp (*A.G.*, p. 3, no. 18); imitation tusks of glass paste, apparently for use on helmets, from the tomb of Spata (*B.C.H.* 2(1878), p. 203); imitation tusks of goat or sheep horn, from Mycenae (*B.S.A.* 25, p. 56).

DEER

Neolithic, physical remains.—*Crete:* Miamù (*A.J.A.* 1897, p. 297); Phaestos (*R.A.L.* 16, p. 265). *Mainland:* Hagia Marina (*R.E.G.* 1912, p. 278). Deer-horn tools were common in Thessalian deposits.

Early Bronze Age, physical remains: Zygouries (*Zygouries*, pp. 27 and 192); Leukas (*Alt-Ithaka*, p. 225); Vardaroftsa (*B.S.A.* 27, p. 45); Hissarlik (*Z. für E. Ver.* 1879, p. 270; *Ilios*, p. 431, nos. 588-590); Saratsé (*B.S.A.* 30, p. 147).

Middle Bronze Age, physical remains: Aspis, date not certain (*B.C.H.* 30(1906), p. 39); Marmariani (*P.T.* p. 54; *D.S.* pl. 45-47, pp. 355-358); Vardaroftsa (*B.S.A.* 27, p. 45); Vardino (*Liverpool Annals* 12, p. 31).

Late Bronze Age.—Crete, physical remains: horns of the roe deer in the Snake Goddess Collection, Knossos (*B.S.A.* 9, p. 41; *P. of M.* 1, p. 496); *Cervus elaphus*, from Tylissos (*Eph.* 1912, p. 231; *Neue Denkschriften* 46(1911), p. 163: these remains were very small in quantity); fallow deer, from the Psychro Cave (*Proceedings of the Manchester Literary and Philosophical Society* 46(1902), p. xlvii; cf. *J.H.* 17(1897), p. 355). *Mainland*, physical remains: Mycenae (*Mycenaean Age*, p. 69; *J.A.I.* 29(1914), p. 125); Vardaroftsa (*B.S.A.* 27, p. 45).

Representations in art: seal from Knossos, showing a deer wounded with a spear or an arrow (*Eph.* 1907, p. 179, pl. 8, no. 125); a seal from Psychro Cave, showing a deer attacked by dogs or lions (*Eph.* 1907, p. 178, pl. 8, no. 116); seal from eastern or central Crete, showing a deer wounded with a spear or arrow (*Eph.* 1907, p. 177, pl. 8, no. 110). Other pictures showing deer attacked by lions indicate either the use of deer in sports of the circus or the residence of Cretans in countries where lions lived in the wild state; *e.g.* a seal from eastern Crete

(*Eph.* 1907, p. 183, pl. 8, no. 152); a seal from the Thisbe collection, showing lions seizing a fallow stag (*J.H.* 45(1925), p. 9, no. 4; the hunting fresco in Tiryns (*Tiryns* 2, p. 132); fresco in Tiryns showing unmolested deer (*Tiryns* 2, pp. 140 ff., figs. 60, 61, 62, and pl. 15 and 16, 2); a seal from Mycenae, showing a hunter in a chariot shooting a fallow deer with a bow (Schliemann, *Mycenae*, p. 223, no. 334; cf. *P. of M.* 1, p. 672); one of the grave stelae from Mycenae, showing a hunter in a chariot and a dog following a deer (Schliemann, *Mycenae*, p. 52, no. 29, and p. 80); and a gem from Thisbe showing a female figure shooting a fallow stag with a bow (*J.H.* 45(1925), p. 21, no. 8). Simple pictures of deer, without significant associations, are fairly common as seal designs.

ELK

Early Minoan.—Vardaroftsa (*B.S.A.* 27, p. 45).

WILD GOAT

Middle Minoan.—Tylissos (*Eph.* 1912, p. 231).

Late Minoan, physical remains: Tylissos (*Eph.* 1912, p. 231; *Neue Denkschriften* 46(1911), p. 162: "Unter den Jagdbaren Tieren spielte offenbar die kretische Wildziege (*Capra aegagrus cretensis*) die Hauptrolle; ihre Reste sind in Tylissos so häufig, dass wir annehmen, dieses Jagdwild sei ziemlich regelmässig eingebracht worden"); Psychro Cave (*J.H.* 17(1897), p. 355; *P. of M.* 1, p. 627); and Hagia Triada (*Neue Denkschriften* 46(1911), p. 146).

Representations in art: The wild goat is, next to the long-horned bull, the most frequent subject for pictures on seal-stones. The following list includes only pictures in which the goat is shown in connection with the hunt: Knossos (*S.M.* p. 22, fig. 11a, and pl. 3, no. 73a; *P. of M.* 1, p. 671, a M.M. III seal showing a dog chasing a wild goat); Knossos, Zapher Papoura cemetery (*Prehistoric Tombs*, p. 29, a painted larnax showing a man catching a wild goat with a lasso); Tylissos (*Eph.* 1912, p. 215, and pl. 15e, no. 5, a seal showing a wild goat wounded in the back with an arrow or spear); Psychro Cave (*J.H.* 17(1897), p. 355, a figurine of a man carrying a wild goat); Zakro (*J.H.* 22(1902), p. 78, pl. 6, no. 15, a seal showing a man and two wild goats); Hagia Triada (*M.A.* 13, p. 36, no. 13); and Spata (*B.C.H.* 2(1878), p. 213 and pl. 16, no. 5, an ivory plaque showing a wild goat being attacked by a dog).

The discovery of a specimen of the true wild goat (*Capra aegagrus*) in Macedonia during the World War (D. Knosuloff, *Zoölogischer Anzeiger* 68(1926), pp. 31-32) has proved the incorrectness of the usual view that the animal exists only in Asia Minor and on some of the Greek islands.

HEDGEHOG

Vardino (*Liverpool Annals* 12, p. 31). A vessel resembling a hedgehog was discovered at Hissarlik (*Troja*, p. 130).

PARTRIDGE AND SIMILAR BIRDS

The familiarity of the Cretans with the partridge, the peacock, and, perhaps, the pheasant, is proved by representations of them in Late Minoan art. None of the pictures, however, shows them in connection with hunting, unless we suppose that the fresco painting from Hagia Triada showing a cat stalking a bird is a hunting scene (*M.A.* 13, p. 58 and pl. 8; *P. of M.* 1, pp. 361 and 369; and Glotz, *Civ. Eg.* p. 195). The best picture is that from the Caravanserai at Knossos, certainly representing partridges (*P. of M.* 2, introduction, p. vii; pp. 109 ff.; frontispiece to vol. 2, part I. Others are Knossos, pictures of a peacock on the wall of the Throne Room (*B.S.A.* 6, p. 40); Phaestos, a sealing showing a bird, perhaps a peacock (*M.A.* 13, p. 36, no. 15); Palaikastro, a peacock-like bird on the lid of a ritual object (*B.S.A.* 10, fig. 7).

RABBIT AND HARE

Neolithic, physical remains: Miamù (*A.J.A.* 1897, p. 297), and Phaestos (*M.A.* 19, p. 151). The bones on the latter site are said to have been broken for the extraction of marrow.

Early Bronze Age.—Hissarlik (Virchow, *Troas,* p. 64).

Late Minoan, physical remains: Sarandari, near Palaikastro (*B.S.A.* 11, p. 294); Krasì Pediados (*A.D.* 1929, p. 124, note 2).

Late Minoan: art, seal-stone from central or eastern Crete showing an eagle attacking a hare (*Eph.* 1907, p. 171, pl. 7, no. 71); sealing from Zakro (*B.S.A.,* 8-9 (1929), p. 168, fig. 188). Hare were probably represented in the Hunting Fresco at Tiryns.

Late Cycladic, physical remains: Thera (*Bulletin de l'Ecole française d'Athènes,* 1870, p. 190): "*lapins.*"

Late Helladic, physical remains: Mycenae (*Mycenaean Age,* p. 69); Thebes (*Eph.* 1909, p. 104); Mesianiki (*Eph.* 1914, p. 102).

Whether the bones in question belong to hare or rabbits cannot be affirmed, since they do not seem to have been examined by zoologists. They are usually described as being the bones of hare. In modern times there are no rabbits in Crete proper, but rabbits are numerous in some of the neighboring islands (*Neue Denkschriften* 46(1911), p. 158) and in Greece.

WATER FOWL

Early Aegean.—Hissarlik (*Z. für E. Ver.* 1879, p. 269; Virchow, *Troas,* pp. 62-63: *Anser cinereus, Anser segetum,* and *Cycnus olor;* and *Ilios,* p. 322: *teal* and *wader*).

Late Minoan, art.—Water fowl were a frequent subject for glyptic and other art, but in most cases the birds have not been identified. Moreover, they may at times represent tame geese. A list of examples would be superfluous here for, although they would show the familiarity of the Cretans with the birds, they would neither furnish evidence in support of the proposition—itself almost certain—that the birds were hunted, nor would they tell us what kinds of water fowl the Cretans distinguished.

2. *Neue Denkschriften* 46(1911), p. 162: "Die damalige Kulturstufe Kretas besass also schon eine ausgiebige Viehzucht; hatte aber daneben die Jagd noch beibehalten, die allerdings nur mit primitiven Waffen betrieben wurde."

3. Weapons, equipment, etc.:

Bows.—Both simple and composite bows were used. The former appears on a steatite relief from Knossos (*B.S.A.* 7, p. 44, fig. 13) and on a seal-stone from Mycenae (Schliemann, *Mycenae,* p. 223, no. 334); Evans believes it the more common type (*B.S.A.* 10, p. 59). On the other hand the association of horns of the wild goat with archery on Cretan tablets and the association of these tablets with remains of arrows (*B.S.A.* 10, pp. 58-59; *S.M.,* p. 44), together with a number of pictures from Minoan art, point to the use of the composite bow (see *Eph.* 1907, pl. 8, no. 109; *J.H.* 1925, p. 21, fig. 24 and p. 22, fig. 25; *P. of M.* 1, p.

197, fig. 145; *B.S.A.* 10, p. 59). The manner of making the composite bow is described in the *Iliad* (IV, 104 ff.), and Odysseus' bow seems to have been of that type (*Odyssey* XXI, 11 and 59). The composite bow, especially that of the recoiling type, is said to be more efficient for its length than the simple bow. Neuberger states that some composite bows of the Sioux Indians are capable of sending an arrow a thousand yards, and of driving one through a bison (Neuberger, *The Technical Arts of the Ancients*, English edition, 1930, pp. 218 f.).

Quantities of arrows were discovered at Knossos near the remains of the chest in which the tablets above referred to were found (*B.S.A.* 10, pp. 58-59). In the Tiryns fresco the boar attacked by dogs had been wounded with an arrow (*Tiryns* 2, pl. 13).

CATS.—Glotz (*Civilisation égéene*, p. 195) expressed the idea that cats were sometimes used in hunting birds. This proposition, apparently based on the fresco from Hagia Triada showing a cat stalking a partridge-like bird (*M.A.* 13, p. 58 and pl. 8; *P. of M.* 1, p. 538, fig. 391) is rather hard to accept.

CHARIOTS.—Women are shown riding to the hunt in a chariot on the Tiryns fresco (*Tiryns* 2, p. 12, restored reproduction in color). On a seal from Mycenae we see a hunter standing in a chariot and shooting at a deer—apparently a fallow deer (Schliemann, *Mycenae*, p. 257, no. 376; cf. *P. of M.* 1, p. 672). One of the grave stelae at Mycenae shows a similar scene (Schliemann, *Mycenae*, p. 80, and p. 24, no. 52).

DOGS.—Actual bones of dogs were found in Neolithic context at Knossos (*P. of M.* 2, p. 10), and at Chaeroneia (*R.E.G.* 1912, p. 264; *Pr.* 1909, p. 124). C. Keller states that the dog represented on a green steatite lid from Mochlos (of Early Minoan date) is a Cretan Hound, a dog famous in Classical times as a boar dog and recommended for that use by Xenophon (*Cyneg.* 10, 1). See *Neue Denkschriften* 46(1911), pp. 136 ff. and *Tiryns* 2, p. 110, fig. 47; 111, 115-116, 123, fig. 55, and pl. 13. Pictures showing dogs attacking wild game are not uncommon in Minoan art; see *Eph.* 1907, p. 178, pl. 8, no. 116; p. 181, pl. 8, no. 140 (dogs attacking deer); *S.M.*, p. 22, fig. 11a, and pl. 3, no. 73a; *B.C.H.* 2(1878), p. 213, and pl. 16, no. 5 (dogs attacking wild goats).

LARIAT.—On a L.M. III painted larnax from the Zapher Papoura cemetery is a crude drawing representing men catching a wild goat with a lasso (*Prehistoric Tombs*, p. 29). A M.M. III seal (*P. of M.* 1, p. 684, fig. 503c) shows a man lassoing a sheep which Evans believed to be a wild sheep. Schliemann found some perforated balls at Hissarlik which, he suggests, may have been lasso rings (*Ilios*, p. 442).

NETS.—The boar-hunt fresco from Tiryns shows a boar caught in a net. Compare this with the use of the net in the capture of bulls as illustrated on the cup from Vapheio (*Eph.* 1889, pl. 9, cup no. 1) and on some seals from Hagia Triada (*B.S.A.* 8-9(1929), pp. 103-104, nos. 60, 61).

SPEARS.—Hunting spears appear in the following: the boar-hunt fresco from Tiryns (*Tiryns* 2, p. 13); a gem from Vapheio (*Eph.* 1889, p. 166, pl. 10, no. 15). Many representations of wounded animals show weapons that may be either spears or arrows. Some seals from Hagia Triada apparently show bulls wounded with spears (*B.S.A.* 8-9(1929), p. 101, nos. 52 and 53, and p. 170, no. 160).

X

THE TRADE IN FOOD

Less spectacular, but more important in providing for the needs of the people than hunting was commerce in food.[1*] In this, as in so many other phases of Aegean culture, we are greatly impeded by the lack of documentary material. It is only possible to set forth the conditions that would give rise to such trade, and some archaeological evidence that confirms the surmises thus reached. Apart from the local trading, which need not detain us, the fundamental difference in the character of Egypt and the Aegean lands would naturally give rise to extensive overseas trade, so that the products of the two areas might supplement each other. Crete produces olives and olive oil in abundance; we have seen that it is likely that it already produced wine in the Early Minoan Age. Egypt produces these things, but not in sufficient quantity to supply its needs; on the other hand there are many articles needed in Crete which can best be supplied by or through Egypt.[2*] Given these conditions, it will be reasonable to suppose that the trade existed, provided that it can be shown that the means for carrying it on were available.[3*]

The very conditions of the spread of the early inhabitants of the Aegean lands presuppose that they possessed boats of some size even in Neolithic times. It is evident that they were able to transport cattle. Boats large enough for that are large enough for the trade which we are considering, and we could fairly suppose that there was commerce between Crete and Egypt, even if we had no reason to believe that some of it may have been carried in Egyptian ships. Pictures of ships of the type used by the early inhabitants of the Cyclades have been preserved.

In later times, at least, extensive harbor works existed, apparently for the trade between Crete and Egypt, in both countries. The Egyptian port was near the later Alexandria; its size indicates a very large volume of traffic.[1] The port at the site now known as Komò seems to have been the Cretan terminal; it was connected with Knossos and other parts of Crete by roads on which four-wheeled vehicles as well as pack animals were used as early as Middle Minoan I.[2] Quantities of large jars, whose remains have been discovered at points along the road between Knossos and Komò, indicate that the trade dealt in oil and, perhaps, in wine. The extensive and elaborate provision for the storage of oil in the palace at Knossos, much beyond the needs even of the king's household, is further evidence that there was a trade in oil and that the royal government en-

---

*Numbers followed by the asterisk and enclosed in parentheses refer to notes at the end of the section; see page 87.
[1]P. of M. 1, pp. 292 ff.
[2]Ibid. 2, pp. 60 ff. and 155 ff.

gaged in it. A Middle Minoan seal from Knossos connects the olive with ships; the Minoan jars discovered in Egypt were scarcely sent there empty. In view of these various facts, that Cretan olive oil was exported to Egypt in Minoan times seems to be proved.

That food was imported from Egypt is likely, but it cannot be positively demonstrated. Evans[3] tells of the identification as Egyptian of certain beans discovered at Knossos; this is evidence of a sort, and the fact that beans are now imported is in itself some indication that similar trade may have been carried on in Minoan times.

There is even less real proof of the existence of a trade in food between Crete, the Cyclades, and the mainland, and between Crete and the East.[4] It is probable, however, that Crete was a distributing center for spices and expensive articles of food. Then, as later, there may well have been a certain amount of transporting of animals by water from island to island; if the animal remains from the Cyclades had been scientifically identified and could be compared with those from Crete and the mainland more light could be thrown on this subject. The apparently local character of the food products found at Thera, despite the Cretan influence in the pottery, seems to indicate that there was no extensive trade in grains, vegetables, and the like among the islands.

NOTES

1. See August Köster: *Schiffahrt und Handelsverkehr des östlichen Mittelmeeres im 3. und 2. Jahrtausend v. Chr.* Köster devotes most of his attention to the better documented phases of commerce, *e.g.*, to that between Egypt and Syria. He recognized the existence of Egyptian-Cretan trade from very early times, but he does not mention a trade in food between those countries, nor does he consider the Cretan trade as a whole to have been so important as that between Egypt and Syria (*Beihefte zum alten Orient*, 1924, pp. 3 ff.).

2. Köster speaks of the existence of an extensive trade in foodstuffs, involving the importation of such commodities as olive oil, wine, and livestock from Syria to Egypt. This would prove that Egypt was a market for such goods, and it permits one more confidence in asserting that Egypt already imported them from Crete also (*loc. cit.*, p. 20).

3. Köster states that the trade between Crete and Egypt was dominated by the Egyptians, and that it was carried on largely in Egyptian ships, until the end of the third millenium B.C. This seems to be in accord with Evans' views about the Egyptian and Libyan influence in Crete in Early Minoan times. Köster, of course, recognizes the existence of the Aegean ship in these early times as the vehicle for local Aegean trade (*loc. cit.*, p. 24).

4. Köster mentions oil and wine as probably being among the articles carried in local Aegean trade (*loc. cit.*, p. 34).

---

[3]*Ibid.*, p. 54.

XI

THE PREPARATION OF FOOD

On the whole, the equipment for preparing and serving food changed little from Neolithic times throughout the entire prehistoric period. It would be possible to prepare a list of numerous pottery types used for that purpose and to determine the age of the oldest examples of each. This has not been attempted; in the first place, it would add little or nothing to our knowledge of how the Aegean peoples actually prepared their food and, in the second place, to have any value such a study would have to be based on a first-hand examination of the original material. I have, therefore, limited my attention to those fixtures and utensils directly connected with some culinary purpose: hearths, ovens, spit-rests, pots, kettles, boilers, strainers, and mills. The hearths of Late Helladic date found on the mainland, e.g. at Korakou,[1] are essentially the same as those found on Neolithic sites. They are built up of clay mixed with stones and sherds, and were used for cooking over an open fire. Sometimes the pots had three legs to hold them up from the fire; often they were simply set upon stones.[2] The great hearth in the palace at Mycenae was simply a large and well-made example of the same kind of hearth. Even these simple hearths do not seem to have been used in Crete from Neolithic to sub-Minoan times, and they were not universally used on the mainland.[3]

There can be no doubt that, in addition to cooking in kettles over the fire, the people of that time roasted meat on the spit. Mosso[4] denied this on the ground that no spits had been discovered. This is a rather poor argument, for the spits may have been of wood, and even if made of bronze, not being the sort of article likely to be preserved in tombs, they would most likely end in the melting pot. On the other hand, spit-rests have been discovered.[5] At Thebes, on the mainland, bones have been found burnt only on the tips as though from roasting over the fire.[6] Moreover, the use of the spit is, a priori, almost inevitable.

Thus it appears that, on the whole, the peoples of the Bronze Age were about as well provided, both in foods and equipment for supplying the table, as were the Greeks of later times. The latter had better ovens, better flour, and yeast—an article which the former may have possessed, although no evidence of its existence in their time has come to light. The Greeks also had hens' eggs and a number of spices probably unknown in the Bronze Age. On the other hand, the earlier peoples may have been

[1]Korakou, pp. 83, 85, 90, and 94.
[2]Ibid., p. 99.
[3]See Bulle, Orchomenos, p. 58.

[4]Excursioni nel Mediterraneo, p. 231.
[5]See B.S.A., Supplementary Papers, No. 1, p. 73.
[6]Eph. 1909, p. 104.

able to bake fairly well in clay vessels, and they certainly had available everything necessary to make satisfactory salads, sauces, and sweetened fruit preserves; to boil, bake, and fry meat, fish, and other sea food; and to prepare well-seasoned stewed vegetables. They could prepare a variety of dishes from milk and cheese.

The staple articles known at all in the Prehistoric Age were, as we have seen, nearly all in use during the early period of the Age of Metals. During that age fancy cooking may have developed; naturally, in the absence of legible written records, we can know nothing of the details. This much can be said: Mutton and pork were the principal meats. With them, and probably forming a more important part of the diet, were eaten a considerable variety of leguminous vegetables. Coarse bread, probably unleavened, was made with wheat or barley meal. Some spices were available to season this food. Like later Mediterranean peoples, the prehistoric Aegean peoples probably prepared many salads with green vegetables, vinegar, and olive oil. They must also have had pickled olives and, as delicacies, certain fruits and nuts, such as apples, pears, plums, pomegranates, and almonds. The more fortunate, we may suppose, ate sweets prepared with honey. As drinks they probably had beer and wine. In addition to these usual foods, the meats were supplemented, and in some places largely supplanted by sea food. Beef was sometimes eaten, though more rarely than mutton and pork—perhaps chiefly in connection with religious festivals. Especially among the upper classes fowl and wild game varied the diet.

From these few facts we can see something of what the food of these peoples must have been. Doubtless, could one know in detail all the recipes and combinations used in the kitchens of the Minoan princes, one could prepare a cookbook in many ways comparable with those of our own day. For this phase of life must have been in keeping with the other phases of life in a culture which was by no means primitive or only a few steps above savagery, but which was, rather, highly developed and ages old.

BIBLIOGRAPHY

BAIKIE, J., *The Sea Kings of Crete*. London, 1910.

BELOCH, G., *Griechische Geschichte*, vol. 1¹, 2nd ed., Berlin, 1912.

BLEGEN, C. W., *Korakou*. Boston and New York, 1921.

————, *Zygouries*. Cambridge, Massachusetts, 1928.

BOISACQ, EMILE, *Dictionnaire étymologique de la Langue grecque*. Paris, 1923.

BOSSERT, H. TH., *Alt-Kreta: Kunst und Kunstgewerbe in ägäischen Kulturkreise*. Berlin, 1921 and 1923.

BROWN, EDWARD, *Poultry Breeding and Production*, vol. 2, New York, 1929.

BULLE, H., "Orchomenos." Published in the *Abhandlungen der kaiserlichen bayerischen Akademie (philosophisch-philologische Klasse)*. Munich, 1909.

BURROWS, R. M., *The Discoveries in Crete*. London, 1907 and 1908.

CHAPOUTIER, FERD, and CHARBONNEAUX, JEAN, *Fouilles exécutées à Mallia*. Paris, 1928.

CURTIUS, E., *Principles of Greek Etymology*, translated by Wilkins and England. London, 1886.

DAREMBERG et SAGLIO, *Dictionnaire des Antiquités grecques et romaines*. Paris, 1877-1918.

DÖRPFELD, W., *Alt-Ithaka*. Munich, 1927.

————, *Troja und Ilion: Ergebnisse der Ausgrabung, 1870-1894*. Athens, 1902.

DUSSAUD, R., *Les Civilisations préhelléniques*, 2nd ed., Paris, 1914.

Eranos Vindobonensis. Vienna, 1893.

EVANS, A. J., *Essai de classification des epoques de la civilisation minoenne*. London, 1906.

————, *Essays in Aegean Archaeology presented to Sir Arthur Evans in honor of his seventy-fifth birthday*. Oxford, 1927.

————, *The Palace of Minos at Knossos,* vols. 1, 2, and 3. London, 1921, 1928, and 1930.

————, *The Prehistoric Tombs of Knossos*. London, 1906.

————, *Scripta Minoa*, vol. 1. Oxford, 1909.

————, *The Shaft Graves and Bee-Hive Tombs of Mycenae*. London, 1929.

EWART, MAX, *Reallexikon der Vorgeschichte*. Berlin, 1924-1929.

FICK, AUGUST, *Vorgriechische Ortsnamen*. Göttingen, 1909.

FIMMEN, D., *Die Kretisch-mykenische Kultur*. Leipzig and Berlin, 1921; 1923.

————, *Zeit und Dauer der kretisch-mykenische Kultur*. Leipzig and Berlin, 1909.

FOUQUÉ, M., *Santorin et ses Eruptions*. Paris, 1879.

FRANKFORT, H., *Studies in the Early Pottery of the Near East,* vols. 1 and 2. London, 1924 and 1927.

FURTWÄNGLER, A., *Die antiken Gemmen*. Berlin, 1900.

FURTWÄNGLER and LOESCHKE, *Mykenischen Vasen*. Berlin, 1886.

GLASGOW, G., *The Minoans*. London, 1923.

GAERTRINGEN, F. HILLER VON, *Thera. Untersuchungen, Vermessungen, und Ausgrabungen in den Jahren 1895-1898*. Berlin, 1904.

GLOTZ, G., *La Civilisation égéenne*. Paris, 1923.

————, *Histoire de la Grèce*, vol. 1. Paris, 1925.

GROPENGIESSER, R., *Die Gräber von Attika der vormykenischen und mykenischen Zeit*. Heidelberg, 1907.

HALL, EDITH H., *The Decorative Art of Crete in the Bronze Age.* Bryn Maur Dissertation, 1907.
————, *Sphoungaras.* Philadelphia, 1912.
————, *Vrokastro.* Philadelphia, 1914.
HALL, H. R., *Aegean Archaeology.* London, 1914.
————, *The Civilisation of Greece in the Bronze Age.* London, 1928.
————, *The Oldest Civilisation of Greece.* London, 1901.
HARLAND, J. P., *Prehistoric Aegina.* Paris, 1925.
HAWES, C. H., and H. B., *Crete, the Forerunner of Greece.* London and New York, 1909.
HAWES, H. B., *Gournià, Vasiliki, and other Prehistoric Sites on the Isthmus of Hierapetra.* Philadelphia, 1909.
HEHN, V., *Kulturpflanzen und Haustiere.* 8th ed., Berlin, 1911.
HOEG, CARSTEN, *Les Saracatsans,* vol. 2, Copenhagen, 1926.
JARDÉ, A., *Les céréales dans l'antiquité grecque.* Paris, 1925.
KAVVADIAS, P., Προϊστορική Ἀρχαιολογία. Athens, 1914.
KELLER, A. G., *Homeric Society.* New York, 1902.
KELLER, O., *Thiere des klassischen Altertums.*
KRETSCHMER, P., *Einleitung in die Geschichte der griechischen Sprache.* Göttingen, 1896.
LAYMON and SLOCUM, *Ducks and Geese.* New York, 1922.
LEWY, *Die semitische Fremdwörter in Griechischen.* Berlin, 1895.
LICHTENBERG, R. VON, *Die ägäische Kultur.* Leipzig, 1911.
MARAGHIANNIS, G., *Antiquités crétoises.* 1st series, Vienna, 1907; 2nd series, Candia, 1912; 3rd series, Candia, 1915.
MARIOLOPOULOS, E. G., *Etude sur le Climat de la Grèce.* Paris, 1925.
MATZ, F., *Die frükretischen Siegel.* Berlin, 1928.
MEILLET, A., *Aperçu d'une histoire de la langue grecque.* Paris, 1913.
MEYER, EDUARD, *Geschichte des Altertums.* Vol. 1^2, 3rd ed., Stuttgart, 1913; vol. 2^2, 3rd ed., 1928.
MEYER, LEO, *Handbuch der griechischen Etymologie.* Leipzig, 1901.
MONTELIUS, O., *La Grèce préclassique.* Stockholm, 1924.
MOSSO, A., *Escursioni nel Mediterraneo e gli Scavi in Creta.* Milan, 1907.
MYLONAS, G., Ἡ Νεολιθικὴ Ἐποχὴ ἐν Ἑλλάδι. Athens, 1928.
————, *Excavations at Olynthus, Part 1, The Neolithic Settlement.* Baltimore, 1929.
NEUBERGER, A., *The Technical Arts of the Ancients.* English ed., London, 1930.
NILLSON, M. P., *The Minoan-Mycenaean Religion and its Survival in Greek Religion.* Lund, 1927.
OULIÉ, MARTHE, *Les animaux dans la peinture de la Crète pré-hellénique.* Paris, 1926.
PAPAVASILOIOS, G., Περὶ τῶν ἐν Εὐβοίᾳ ἀρχαίων τάφων. Athens, 1910.
PAULY-WISSOWA, *Realenzyklopädie,* 1894—.
PERROT, G., and CHIPIEZ, CH., *Histoire de l'Art dans l'Antiquité,* vol. 6, Paris, 1893.
PERSSON, A. W., *Kungagraven i Dendra.* Stockholm, 1928.
PHILIPPSON, E., *Das Mittelmeergebeit.* Berlin, 1914.
Phylakopi, Society for the Promotion of Hellenic Studies, Supplementary Paper, No. 4. London, 1904.
POTT, A. F., *Die Personennamen.* Leipzig, 1859.
REISINGER, E., *Kretische Vasenmalerei.* Leipzig, 1912.

RIDGEWAY, *The Early Age of Greece*. Cambridge, 1901.
RODENWALDT, G., *Tiryns,* vol. 2. Halle, 1911.
SCHLIEMANN, H., *Mycenae*. New York, 1880.
————, *Ilios*. New York, 1878.
————, *Tiryns*. New York, 1885.
————, *Troja*. New York, 1884.
SEAGER, R., *Explorations in the Island of Mochlos*. New York, 1912.
————, *The Cemetery of Pachyammos, Crete*. Philadelphia, 1916.
————, *Excavations in the Island of Pseira*. Philadelphia, 1910.
————, *Excavations at Vasiliki*. (Transactions of the Department of Archaeology of the University of Pennsylvania.) Philadelphia, 1905.
THUMB, A., *Handbuch der neugriechischen Volkssprache*. Strassburg, 1910.
TREVOR, BATTYE, *Camping in Crete*. London, 1913.
TSOUNTAS, CHR., Αἱ προιστορικαὶ Ακροπολεις Διμηνίου καὶ Σέσκλου. Athens, 1908.
TSOUNTAS and MANATT, *The Mycenaean Age*. Boston, 1927.
WACE and THOMPSON, *Prehistoric Thessaly*. Cambridge, 1912.
XANTHOUDIDES, St., *The Vaulted Tombs of Mesarà*. London, 1924.

ABBREVIATIONS

A.D...............................'Αρχαιλογικὸν Δελτίον.
A.G.............................FÜRTWÄNGLER: *Die Antiken Gemmen*.
A.J.A...............................*American Journal of Archaelogy*.
Alt-Ithaka ....DÖRPFELD: *Alt-Ithaka*.
Årberättelse....................*Humanist Vetanskapsfundet i Lund, Årberättelse*
Arch. für Rel. ....*Archif für Religionswissenschaft*.
Annuario della r. sc. Atene......*Annuario della reale scuola archeologica italiana in Atene*.
B.C.H...........................*Bulletin de Correspondence hellénique*.
Bronze Age.....................HALL.: *Civilisation of Greece in the Bronze Age*.
B.S.A...........................*Annals of the British School at Athens*.
Civ. Eg.......................GLOTZ: *La Civilisation égéenne*.
Civilisations préhelléniques ......DUSSAUD: *Les Civilisations préhelléniques*.
Daremberg et Saglio ....*Dictionnaire des Antiquités grecques et romaines*.
Dict. Etym.....................BOISACQ: *Dictionnaire étymologique de la langue grecque*.
D.S................................Αἱ Προιστορικαὶ 'Ακροπόλεις Διμινίου καὶ Σεσκλου.
Eph...............................'Αρχαιολογικὴ 'Εφημερίς.
Euboea........................Περὶ τῶν ἐν Εὐβοίᾳ ἀρχαίων τάφων.
G. des A. ....MEYER: *Geschichte des Altertums*.
Gournià........................HAWES: *Gournià*.
Ilios............................SCHLIEMANN: *Ilios*.
J.A.I............................*Jahrbuch des deutschen archäologischen Instituts*.
J.A.I. Anzeiger.................*Archäologischer Anzeiger*.
J.H............................*Journal of Hellenic Studies*.
J.O.E.I.........................*Jahreshefte des österreichischen archäoligischen Instituts*.

Korakou........................BLEGEN: *Korakou.*
Klio............................*Beitrage zur alten Geschichte.*
Liverpool Annals................*Annals of the Liverpool University.*
M.A............................*Monumenti Antichi.*
M.A.I..........................*Mitteilungen des deutschen archäologischen In-stituts, athenische Abteilung.*
Mallia.........................CHAPOUTIER et CHARBONNEAUX: *Fouilles exécu-tées à Mallia.*
Mem. r. Ist. lomb. ....*Memorie del reale Istituto lombardo, classe di lettere, scienze morali, e storiche.*
Mesarà.........................XANTHOUDIDES: *The Vaulted Tombs of Mesarà.*
Mittelmeergebiet...............PHILIPPSON: *Das Mittelmeergebiet.*
Mycenaean Age..................TSOUNTAS and MANATT: *The Mycenaean Age.*
Neue Denkschriften.............*Neue Denkschriften der Schweizerischen Gesell-schaft für die gesamten Naturwissenschaften.*
Olynthus.......................MYLONAS: *The Excavations at Olynthus, Part I, the Neolithic Settlement.*
Orchomenos ....BULLE: *Orchomenos.*
P. of M........................EVANS: *The Palace of Minos at Knossos.*
Phylakopi......................*Society for the Promotion of Hellenic Studies, Supplementary Paper, No. 4.*
Pr.............................Πρακτικὰ τῆς ἐν Ἀθήναις ἀρχαιολογικῆς Ἑταιρίας.
Prehistoric Tombs..............EVANS: *The Prehistoric Tombs of Knossos.*
Pseira.........................R. SEAGER: *Excavations in the Island of Pseira.*
P.T............................WACE and THOMPSON: *Prehistoric Thessaly.*
P.W............................PAULY-WISSOWA: *Realenzyklopädie.*
R.A............................*Revue Archéologique.*
R.A.L..........................*Rendiconti della reale Accademia dei Lincei.*
R.E.A..........................*Revue des Etudes anciennes.*
R.E.G..........................*Revue des Etudes grecques.*
R.V.G..........................*Reallexikon der Vorgeschichte.*
Santorin.......................FOUQUÉ: *Santorin et ses Eruptions.*
S.M............................EVANS: *Scripta Minoa.*
Sphoungaras....................HALL: *Sphoungaras.*
Troas..........................VIRCHOW: *Troas.*
Troja..........................SCHLIEMANN: *Troja.*
Tiryns.........................SCHLIEMANN: *Tiryns.*
Tiryns 2.......................RODENWALDT: *Tiryns, vol. 2.*
Z. für E. ....*Zeitschrift für Ethnologie.*
Zygouries......................BLEGEN: *Zygouries.*

PERIODICALS

Akademie der Wissenschaften zu Berlin, Abhandlungen.
American Journal of Archaeology.
Annual of the British School at Athens.
Antiquaries' Journal.
Antiquity.
'Αρχαιολογικὴ 'Εφημερίς.
Archaeologia.
'Αρχαιολογικὸν Δελτίον.
Archif für Religionswissenschaft.
Art and Archaeology.
Ausonia.
Bulletin de Correspondence hellénique.
Bulletin de l'Ecole française d'Athenes.
Classical Journal.
Classical Philology.
Humanist Vetanskapsfundet i Lund, Årberättelse = Bulletin de la Société des Lettres de Lund.
Jahrbuch des deutschen archäologischen Instituts, bound with the Archäologischer Anzeiger.
Jahreshefte des österreichischen archäologischen Instituts.
Journal of Egyptian Archaeology.
Journal of Hellenic Studies.
Klio: Beitrage zur alten Geschichte.
Liverpool University, Annals.
Memorie del reale Istituto lombardo, Classe di lettere, scienze morali, e storiche.
Memoirs and Proceedings of the Manchester Literary and Philosophical Society.
Mitteilungen des deutschen archäoligischen Instituts, athenische Abteilung.
Monumenti antichi.
National Geographic Magazine.
Der Naturforscher.
Neue Denkschriften der schweizerischen Gesellschaft für die gesamten Naturwissenschaften.
Petermanns Mitteilungen.
Πρακτικὰ τῆς ἐν 'Αθήναις ἀρχαιολογικῆς 'Εταιρίας.
Reale Scuola archeologica italiana in Atene, Annuario.
Rendiconti della reale accademia dei Lincei.
Revue archéologique.
Revue des Etudes anciennes.
Revue des Etudes grecques.
Verhandlungen der berliner Gesellschaft für Erdkunde.
Vierteljahresschrift der naturforschenden Gesellschaft in Zurich.
Zeitschrift für Ethnologie.
Zoölogischer Anzeiger.

INDEX

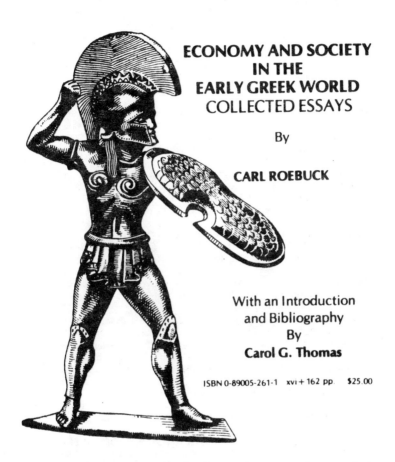

ECONOMY AND SOCIETY IN THE EARLY GREEK WORLD
COLLECTED ESSAYS

By

CARL ROEBUCK

With an Introduction
and Bibliography
By
Carol G. Thomas

ISBN 0-89005-261-1   xvi + 162 pp. $25.00

" In the preface to his *Ionian Trade and Colonization,* Carl A. Roebuck succinctly describes the principal themes which he has pursued throughout a long and scholarly career: "I found myself grappling with two problems of early Greek history which have been the subject of recent controversy, how to assess the economic factor and how to define the role of Ionia." Few scholars have so thoroughly investigated the development of Ionia, especially its economic base, from the migrations in the early Dark Age to the period of the Persian Wars. Yet Professor Roebuck has always recognized that a society is far more than its economic system and that Ionia must be placed in the larger context of Greece as a whole. Hence his work has looked beyond Ionia and economics to the entire world of early Greece and has illuminated particularly the emergence of the distinctive product of the Dark and Archaic ages, the *polis.*

From the *Preface* by Carol G. Thomas

PAPERBACK

Bell, H.I., CULTS & CREEDS IN GRAECO-ROMAN EGYPT, 128 pp. ISBN 0-89005-088-0 .... $6.00

Budge, E.A. Wallis, EGYPTIAN LANGUAGE, 256 pp. ISBN 0-89005-095-3. .... $6.00

Budge, E.A. Wallis, HERB-DOCTORS AND PHYSICIANS IN THE ANCIENT WORLD: The Divine Origin of the Craft of the Herbalist, 104 pp. ISBN 0-89005-252-2. .... $6.00

Buschor, Ernst, GREEK VASE PAINTING. Trans by G.C. Richards with a preface by Percy Gardner. xii + 180 pp. ISBN 0-89005-267-0. Limited Quantity. $7.50

Cheesman, G.L., AUXILIA OF THE ROMAN IMPERIAL ARMY, 192 pp. ISBN 0-89005-096-1 .... $6.00

*Cornford, F.M., MICROCOSMOGRAPHIA ACADEMICA, 64 pp. ISBN 0-89005-318-9 .... $3.00

Gardiner, Alan H., CATALOGUE OF THE EGYPTIAN HIEROGLYPHIC & PRINTING TYPE, 45 pp., ISBN 0-89005-098-8 .... $6.00

Griffith, G.T., THE MERCENARIES OF THE HELLENISTIC WORLD, 350 pp. ISBN 0-89005-085-6 .... $6.00

Hirth, F., CHINA AND THE ROMAN ORIENT, 362 pp. ISBN 0-89005-093-7 .... $6.00

*Miller, S., (ed.), A R E T E, Ancient writers, papyri, and inscriptions on the History and Ideals of Greek Athletics and Games. 128 pp. ISBN 0-89005-313-8 .... $7.50

Newberry, P.E., ANCIENT EGYPTIAN SCARABS, 264 pp. ISBN 0-89005-092-9 .... $6.00

*Pendlebury, J.D.S., A HANDBOOK TO THE PALACE OF MINOS AT KNOSSOS. With an Introduction and Bibliography by Leslie Preston Day. 89 pp. + 15 plates + 9 plans. ISBN 0-89005-312-x $8.50

Petrie, Flinders, TEN YEARS DIGGING IN EGYPT, 250 pp. ISBN 0-89005-107-0 .... $6.00

Petrie, Flinders, HISTORICAL SCARABS, 84 pp., incl. 69 pl. ISBN 0-89005-122-4 .... $5.00

Robinson, R., SOURCES FOR THE HISTORY OF GREEK ATHLETICS, xii + 289 pp. ISBN 0-89005-297-2 ...... $7.50

Schoder, R.V., MASTERPIECES OF GREEK ART. 120 pp. + 96 color plates. ISBN 0-89005-071-0. (All Sales Final) $6.00

Sturtevant, E.H., THE PRONUNCIATION OF GREEK & LATIN, 192 pp. ISBN 0-89005-087-2 .... $6.00

Tarn, W.W., HELLENISTIC MILITARY & NAVAL DEVELOPMENTS, 178 pp. ISBN 0-89005-086-4 .... $6.00

Thompson, E.M., HANDBOOK OF GREEK & LATIN PALEOGRAPHY, ISBN 0-89005-094-5 .... $6.00

Whibley, L. GREEK OLIGARCHIES, 224 pp. ISBN 0-89005-091-0 .... $6.00

Zielinski, Th., THE RELIGION OF ANCIENT GREECE, 248 pp. ISBN 0-89005-090-2 .... $6.00

*NEW

ARES PUBLISHERS Inc.
612 NORTH MICHIGAN AVE., SUITE 216
CHICAGO, ILLINOIS 60611